The
Twin Flame Guidebook:

Your Practical Guide to Navigating the Journey

Book Two

By K.D. Courage

This book is designed to provide information and inspiration to our readers. It is sold with the understanding that the publisher is not engaged to render any type of psychological, legal, or any other kind of professional or other advice. The content is the sole expression and opinion of its author, and not necessarily that of the publisher. No warranties or guarantees are expressed or implied by the publisher's choice to include any of the content in this volume. Neither the publisher nor the author(s) shall be liable for any physical, psychological, emotional, financial, or commercial damages, including, but not limited to, special, incidental, consequential or other damages. Our views and rights are the same: You are responsible for your own choices, actions, and results.

Some names and identifying details have been changed to protect the privacy of individuals. The author has tried to recreate events, locations, and conversations from her memories of them. In order to maintain anonymity in some instances, she has changed the names of individuals and places and she may have changed some identifying characteristics and details. Although the author/publisher have made every effort to ensure that the information in this book was correct at press time, the author and publisher do not assume and hereby disclaim any liability to any party for any loss, damage, or disruption caused by errors or omissions, whether such errors or omissions result from negligence, accident, or any other cause.

Acknowledgements

First, I'd like to thank my beautiful Divine Counterpart, my Ascension Partner, the one who has lit me up from the inside out, tossed my world upside down in the most beautiful of ways, and who has co-created this Journey with me. Without you, I'd still be living my ordinary, three-dimensional (3-D) experience and while that was great in many ways and part of my life path (and I might add, chock-full of all the lessons I needed for my Soul Growth), I am looking forward to the next chapters with newly awakened eyes and ever-expanding perspectives of me, of unconditional love, and of how wonderful this world—and this human experience—can truly be.

I know you don't like labels. I know you say you do not believe in this Journey, and that is okay. You don't have to agree with my perspective. I fully recognize and respect you have your own views and your own beliefs, and you have your own life path and choices to make and you, of course, have Free Will. I honor and respect all of that and have learned to release and surrender to this process and to accept whatever may unfold for me, now and into the future, for I know it is always in the best and highest good for all.

My truth is that...though you may be unaware, you've opened my eyes in every conceivable way, and you've introduced me to the concept of true and unconditional love. I admire and call upon your intelligence, your fierceness, your fiery energy, your strength, and your propensity for unparalleled boundary-setting when I most needed those qualities. You've shown me so much of the things I needed to see and experience in order to develop and grow in wonderful (if not always comfortable) ways. My truth is that you're the yin to my yang, the night to my day, the sun to my moon, the paint to my canvas. You bring light, life, love, joy, sparkle, fun, and color to everything you do, and I am in awe of all the magic you create. Truly, you are "Gold."

"Gold (gold)
Always believe in your soul
You've got the power to know
You're indestructible, always believing
You are gold (gold)
Glad that you're bound to return
There's something I could have learned
You're indestructible, always believing..."

"Gold" by Spandau Ballet

One day, my hope is that we truly have that "blank page" moment once again where we can set it all down and release it, but again, I know I must accept whatever comes my way. I do forgive everything that transpired, and I do hope you will forgive me for it all, too. Not the least of which was not respecting your boundaries. I've learned so much. But alas, my unconditional love and respect endures.

An acknowledgement wouldn't be complete, of course, without thanking God/Universe/Source Energy who makes everything, all of creation, every creation, possible. I am very grateful for my renewed (and growing) connection to you and to the Divine realms. Every day brings new guidance, new insights, new vision, and the ability to see the world and every experience I have with "new eyes."

Thank you, too, to my Mom and my Dad and to my kids. You all are my anchor, my support, my life, my love. Whatever idea or project I ever came up with, or dragged you all off to do over the years, you were always supportive. I'd like to thank you and I hope you had a few happy adventures along the way with me, too. One thing for sure, it's never been boring. Just wait and see what we will do next! To my children, I am so very proud of you and who you are, and who you are becoming. May you always reach for your full potential in life and in every endeavor, and may you be blessed in every way.

I'd also like to thank my dear friends, so many, too many to name here, but I'd like to especially thank: Sylvia Escalante (The Enchanted World of Twin Flame), my wonderful creative partner, spiritual teacher, and fellow author, as well as: Brian Harrison Mack (screenwriter and personal friend); K Moon (Western astrologer); Elizabeth Grove (Paranormal Priestess); Lee & Sherry Patterson (Relationship Reinvented); Magenta Pixie; Bracha Goldsmith; Melissa Parks (intuitive); Susan Lathers (past life readings), and all the awe-inspiring friends I've made on this Journey all over this gorgeous world, including, but not limited to: Stephanie in Denver and Ang in London, and all my new friends and fans across social media. Though I cannot personally answer every email or message, just know I am right there with you. We're in this together, and you're never alone. I hope my books will help you on your Journey and your spiritual path and my goal, as always, is to leave the planet a little better than I found it.

I'd also like to thank the other stellar professionals who make this all happen with me: Chelsea Fone (graphic designer who also provides creative oversight and direction); Nick Caya, Mary, and all the folks at Word2Kindle.com who make the books look oh-so-sharp, and all the people and places who supply me with coffee, inspiration, copies, Kleenex, craft beers, and champagne.

Truly, I love and adore you all.

K.D. Courage (*July 2020*)

Table of Contents

Prologue

In Book One of *The Twin Flame Guidebook: Your Practical Guide to Navigating the Journey*, I was attempting to process and understand the Journey in my own way, and in capturing my thoughts on paper (er, on the screen), it occurred to me that the information *might* be useful to others.

Indeed it has, as the first book is selling well all over the world, and the publishing company that I started to get the first book out into the world is doing well and leading me further along my life purpose and mission, and for all of that, I am extremely grateful to God/Universe/Source Energy, and to each and every one of you. Before you dive into the pages of this book, I just wanted to highlight some of Book One so you will have a foundational understanding to set the stage for your reading and understanding of this second book in the series. (And if you have a chance, please purchase and read that book, as well. It's available on both Amazon, and Barnes & Noble, as well as select retail outlets worldwide. I also appreciate reviews on whatever platform you purchase the book and also on Goodreads. Thank you in advance!)

In Book One—as I described my own personal Journey of leaving a karmic partner of 20 years and embarking on the many aspects of the Twin Flame Journey—we:

- Explored the origins of Twin Flames
- Discovered how to know if the person you've met is your Twin Flame
- Dived into the roles of the Divine Feminine and the Divine Masculine
- Learned the basic stages associated with the Twin Flame Journey
- Explored karma and the role of karmic soulmates
- Talked about synchronicities, miracles, and the mysterious red thread
- Touched on Twin Flame telepathy, astral sex, and more.

I also wanted to point out that though the book is selling briskly all over the world, my orientation is of the Episcopalian faith, so there are Biblical references throughout. I want to state for the record that I am deeply respectful of all world religions, and indeed, there are many beautiful commonalities amongst all of them. I am sure that, if you are not Christian, there are beautiful passages from your own religious texts that will help support the premises contained within this book. Please feel free to email me at: TwinFlameGuidebook@ gmail.com if you would like to help me gain a greater, more holistic understanding.

In closing, as you go along your own Journey and your spiritual path, may you remember that out of total devastation and destruction is born the light. Just like the Phoenix, may we all rise up from the ashes toward the highest potential and fulfillment of our best selves, the ones who will lead the world into a new understanding and new templates of unconditional love, spiritually rooted relationships, and deep connection.

What is Unconditional Love?

Of course, unconditional love is the foundation of the entire Twin Flame/Divine Counterpart Journey, and it deserves the marquee spot in this book. If you haven't discovered it yet, or if you're new to the Journey, you're in for a treat. It will break you, it will make you, and you'll never see the world through the same eyes again.

To delve further into the concept, into the emotion, of unconditional love, the best and most simplistic words I have ever read or heard on the subject comes to us from the Bible in 1 Corinthians 13:4-7: *"Love is patient, love is kind. It does not envy, it does not boast, it is not proud. It does not dishonor others, it is not self-seeking, it is not easily angered, it keeps no record of wrongs. Love does not delight in evil, but rejoices with the truth. It always protects, always trusts, always hopes, always perseveres. (NIV)"*

Unconditional love is, simply, love without boundaries, without restrictions. It is about expansion. It is a state in which a person has the ability to express freely the emotion of love without fear, without hesitation, and without any strings attached to it.

It means that no matter what one does to you, the love between you doesn't go away. It stays, it remains, and perhaps even grows and deepens.

But what if someone slights you with words or cuts you to the bone with words or actions? What if they say the words you least wanted to hear, EVER? Words that even on a subconscious level, you knew you never wanted to hear (words that you didn't even realize *could* cut you to the bone). Words and phrases that hurt you more deeply than anyone or anything ever could? This happens frequently in Twin Flame relationships when Twin Flames "trigger" one another.

It means your love for that person…it does not dissipate or fade away. You don't retract it or withhold it when certain conditions are not met. You "feel" into it and let it continue to overtake you and flow through you and within you, even as you are experiencing the hurts or slights. You soften your heart and your approach, even when everything in you wants to harden, even when your head screams to protect yourself.

You express your unconditional love to the other person and let them know they are "safe" with you, no matter what. And you make it clear that they know that no matter what they do or say (now or in the future), that you love them completely… and unconditionally. This love was given to them freely when you met or over time and unconditional love, never will, and never can be taken away.

There is another passage in the Bible that touches on the nature of God's love for us and the example it sets for us in all our worldly relationships. Allow this love to be infused in you, to flow within you, and from you. Practice it daily, no matter where you are, whether you are at the grocery store, at work, whether you are stuck in traffic, or you're staring out the window watching a neighbor let their dog poop on your grass. It doesn't have to mean you are a doormat, though. You can stand up for yourself and set your boundaries, but you can still treat all people—even the ones you don't like right off the bat—with dignity and kindness.

This passage comes from *Jeremiah 31:3*, and it states:

The Lord has appeared of old to me, saying: "Yes, I have loved you with an everlasting love; Therefore, with lovingkindness I have drawn you." (NKJV)

Lovingkindness. Love infused with grace and compassion, the golden side of the coin. On the flip side of the coin, perhaps the silver side, there is fear. In every relationship you have and experience in your lifetime, your relationship will be set to one side of the coin or the other. Either love, or fear.

In a toxic relationship, one where you begin to realize your needs are not known or met, when you realize that the other person has many conditions, in fact, for loving you, you begin to realize that's not truly love. If there's fear there, that's not love. At least, that was the case for me. The two cannot co-exist.

Take a look at this quote from *1 John 4:18*:

There is no fear in love. But perfect love drives out fear, because fear has to do with punishment. The one who fears is not made perfect in love. (NIV)

Unconditional love also means there is no room for resentment. You cannot hold unconditional love for a person and also hold resentment toward them for something they have said or done.

So, if you are holding resentment toward someone, release that resentment. How do you do that? By willing it so, and making that choice. But you can also use the ancient Hawaiian practice of **Ho'oponopono**, a practice of reconciliation and forgiveness. This word can be translated to "fix a mistake," or "make it right."

There are four basic steps to Ho'oponopono. Think of the person you want to offer forgiveness to, whether it is your Self, your Twin Flame, your partner, your spouse, your ex-spouse, your parent, your children, your friend or friends, your mechanic, your co-worker, a politician, or anyone who has harmed you in any way, large or small. Think of the person and state their name and then slowly say these words, taking them in as you say each statement. Even if you don't feel the "I love you." Even if you're still angry or resentful. Just say the words. It will wash it all away…all the hurt, all the anger, all the resentment. If it doesn't, then repeat until it feels better. It works. I promise.

Ho'oponopono Forgiveness Prayer

"I love you."

"I'm sorry."

"Please forgive me."

"Thank you."

The Truth About Energetic Chasing

So, if you are at the point in your Journey where your Twin has either blocked you on social media and/or asked you to please stop contacting them, then you may be entering another Dark Night of the Soul.

This is a perfectly normal and common occurrence on the Twin Flame Journey.

It can be unnerving, though, when you, as the "chaser," experience such a strong connection with your Twin Flame. You think to yourself: How can this *not* be true? How can my Twin not feel these feelings, these emotions, this connection, to the extent I am feeling it? How is he or she missing all the synchronicities that I am seeing (or not admitting to seeing them)? How come he or she won't admit to having feelings for me?

The three-dimensional (3-D) answer is simple. It is this: Respect the person and do as they ask. If they ask you to stop contacting them via phone, email, or social media, then you need to do that. Pushing it only makes it worse and makes you seem more "unhinged." This is tough because it feels like you must continue with the pushing, or you feel you are abandoning your Journey, or letting the Universe/ Source Energy down. You feel you must do anything in your power to make the connection happen in the 3-D, to bring your Divine Union "down" into this material plane.

I talk a bit about this in the chapter of *The Twin Flame Guidebook*: "Why We as Divine Feminines Chase." There are many reasons we are driven to act in these ways, and let me tell you, I have probably made every "mistake" in the book with my Twin. The intent was never of "mal-intent," but I'm afraid it perhaps came off that way to my Twin. That is a bitter pill to swallow.

I have received some really critical messages from my guides. They've asked me to stop chasing my Twin mentally for the foreseeable future. I asked them whether I should withdraw my energy from her entirely, and the answer back to me was "no." But they do want me to shift at least my mental energy away from my Twin. I did not know this, but apparently, the mental energy can be very strong and almost overwhelming, particularly for a Twin who can feel you in his or her energy field. (One of the additional lessons of this Journey is the tremendous power, the enormous power, that we wield. Often, it doesn't feel like that in the 3-D, but we do.)

I asked the guides for help with this request to shift my mental energy away from my Twin, who also happens to be female, and from the connection because I am going to need it. I asked the guides if they know how difficult this assignment, this request will be, and they acknowledged, yes, it will be very difficult.

This Twin Flame Journey, when you step back from it, can seem very addictive at times. Like, if you're missing your Twin, you take a "virtual hit" or a "virtual bump" every time you think about them. Or when you search and find a new video on YouTube describing the exact emotions you have at that moment. When you go out and Google someone, or try to look at their social media accounts, as many do. When you spend countless hours on the Journey, thinking about it, researching it, doing the things we do, reading, watching, searching. While it's not 3-D contact, it's still chasing, nonetheless.

I asked for help with my particular situation, so while I was taking a brief nap to recover from the work of the day in the early afternoon, these messages came to me, as they often do when I am in the dreamspace.

"This" (meaning the break from thinking of her that I've been asked to take, along with the entire Journey) "is a 'covenant' or an agreement." (The guides were referring to their request of me turning my mental attention and energy away from my Twin.) Interesting that they used the Biblical word: Covenant. I looked this up because I wanted to understand the word on a much deeper level.

The word "covenant," infrequently heard in conversation, is quite commonly used in legal, social (marriage), and religious and theological contexts.

The Idea of Covenant. The term "covenant" is of Latin origin (con venire), meaning a coming together. It presupposes two or more parties who come together to make a contract, agreeing on promises, stipulations, privileges, and responsibilities. In religious and theological circles there has not been agreement on precisely what is to be understood by the biblical term. It is used variously in biblical contexts. In political situations, it can be translated treaty; in a social setting, it means a lifelong friendship agreement; or it can refer to a marriage.

The Biblical words most often translated "covenant" are "berit" in the Old Testament (appearing about 280 times) and diatheke in the New Testament (at least 33 times). The preferred meaning of this Old Testament word is bond; a covenant refers to two or more parties bound together. The New Testament word for covenant has usually been translated as covenant, but testimony and testament have also been used. This Greek word basically means to order or dispose for oneself or another.

The generally accepted idea of binding or establishing a bond between two parties is supported by the use of the term berit [tyir.B]. When Abimelech and Isaac decided to settle their land dispute, they made a binding agreement, league, or covenant to live in peace. An oath confirmed it (Genesis 26:26-31). Joshua and the Gibeonites bound themselves, by oath, to live in peace together (Joshua 9:15), although Yahweh commanded that Israel was not to bind themselves to the people living in the land of Canaan (Deuteronomy 7:2; Judges 2:2). Solomon and Hiram made a binding agreement to live and work in peace together (1 Kings 5:12). A friendship bond was sealed by oath between David and Jonathan (1 Samuel 20:3 1 Samuel 20:16-17). Marriage is also a bond (covenant) for life.

The covenants referred to above were between two equal parties; this means that the covenant relationship was bilateral. The bond was sealed by both parties vowing, often by oath, that each, having equal privileges and responsibilities, would carry out their assigned roles.

- *From https://www.biblestudytools.com/dictionary/covenant/*

The guides then went on to tell me that I "agreed to this." I agreed to the Separation covenant with my Twin in a time and space that seems very far from this one, and very close all at the same time. There were "assigned roles." My role, as I currently understand it, has been not only to love openly and fiercely in the 3-D and to acknowledge the connection fully, but also to push the limits of this unconventional relationship or connection. My Twin's role has been to trigger me at key steps of the way, reflecting all my insecurities and all my wounds, projecting them right back onto me so I could see them, view them, acknowledge, purge, and heal them. In turn, I have done the same to her and for her. It seems I know how to trigger her perfectly, every time, unwittingly. She does the same to me. This latest request for me to withdraw is all part of the "master plan," the choreography of this dance between my Twin and me. She needs me to pull back, so that she can experience what I experienced when I was first awakened to this connection, and she was asleep to it. Even the deep separations and "no contact" periods, it is believed, are planned out well in advance so that each of you can do the necessary healing work, the work of bringing the subconscious to the conscious and then again, healing and transmuting your core wounds, hurts, and traumas.

The guides went on to tell me that if I "master my mind and thoughts, then the sky is the limit."

Throughout this Journey, we've had to learn to master so many lessons...our perception of ourselves, recognizing all our core wounds and triggers, fully realizing the love we have not only for our Twins, but for ourselves, all while managing our emotions, managing our actions, and exponentially increasing our understanding of true, unconditional love.

And now, here's a new, big lesson, a brand-new assignment, right in front of me, and that is I must learn to control my mind and be disciplined with my thoughts. When I think about that, as a somewhat undisciplined person, it feels strange and uncomfortable.

But then I think about a person, for example, who is training for a marathon, or training for American Ninja Warrior (as another example), and that requires not only commitment, but extreme focus and discipline. While my example is focused on the body, it makes sense to me that our guides would want us to be masters of thought, as well. For when we can master our thoughts, we can master our futures and shape our own realities. We will no longer be the victim of negative thoughts, whether in our Journeys or in life in general. We will no longer be someone that life "happens to." We will make it happen. We will forge a new way, a better, lighter, brighter way for ourselves, whether that includes our Twin in our 3-D future, or not.

Only time will tell where this latest lesson will lead me. But I am looking forward to trying. And I know on some days, I will fail colossally. But that's ok. I am still human. I am still learning, still growing.

I still love my Twin, my Divine Counterpart (whatever label one would want to attach to it) with all my heart, but this time is intended for me to turn my focus to myself and love myself and follow my own heart, my own wishes and pursuits, independent of my Twin. Truly it is time for me to "do me" (as my Twin once said). It also releases me possibly from the last throes of co-dependency and those patterns, both with my karmic partner and with my Twin. Incidentally, I never thought I was co-dependent, until I read a book on it (a very good one called "The Language of Letting Go" by Melody Beattie), and I realized I had become a "textbook case," in some ways.

I am sure this is not the LAST lesson for me, because according to Abraham Hicks, the learning, the work…is never completely done.

As I've stated before, this work, these lessons, are a "daily unfolding." I believe that all there is left for me to do now is to be not only a good student, but a good soldier…as we continue to advance forward as part of God's Army of Love.

Sea Life

On a beautiful fall day, I walked down to the water's edge. The water where I live, part-time in Florida, was five different shades of blue, from teal to cerulean to deep blue. A seagull swooped over the water's surface. The water, smooth as a pane of glass, seemed static like nothing was going on under the surface. But then, as I watched, tiny bubbles of life started teeming under the waterline. Little gills batted against the water, making tiny ripples and waves that danced together under a sunbeam. Contrary to what the eye could perceive, there was so much going on just underneath the lip of the water. Things are way beyond what can be seen.

It struck me that our Journey is just like that. One Twin, the seagull circling above the surface, lonely, eyeing for any sign or signal of life. The other Twin, submerged, below the surface, a perfect balance. One above, one below. The seagull in the bright light of day, the other Twin, like a beautiful fish, swimming in the obscure light…deep twilight water, the color of night, with only beams of sunlight dancing over the fish from time to time. They exist symbiotically, each portraying the role he or she was meant to play. In perfect natural harmony.

The one thing that is missing from this comparison is the human angst of emotion trying to force the connection one way or another, rather than dancing with it like a cattail moved by the sea breeze. Prior to this walk, I thought I had known what surrender means. Many months ago, I proudly stated to myself, "That's it. I have completely surrendered to the Journey."

That couldn't have been more wrong because it took another round of brutal triggering between me and my Twin, that tit-a-tat, that back-and-forth, the push-pull, and the perfect triggering of the other that only true Twins can do to one another. Your greatest fear, your greatest vulnerability, the thing or things you despise (or fear) the most will be called out to you. And you will reflect back to your Twin his or her biggest fears and insecurities. You won't mean to, but you will. It's a given. On this Journey, it's part of the natural order of things.

It took this colossal emotional tsunami to surface even more things that needed to be acknowledged, purged, and healed. In fact, I am still processing it all and will be for the foreseeable future. I am a villager, washed up onto the shore by this force of nature, crumpled up like a sun-bleached tiki bar receipt. I have been stripped of my self-image, my self-confidence, my false, ego-driven mask of bravado, and I am ... back to my basic essence ... like a small child just starting out on her life's journey.

Anything I thought I was, anything I thought was important, any success I might have eeked out over 40-plus years has ceased to be. And now, it's just me.

Once everything is stripped away, and you're left with just yourself...well, then, that's all you've got to work with. There's nothing else left to focus on. There's no other person to attach yourself to, or another concept. It's just you, looking back in the mirror at you. The only project ahead is you. The future you see is...simply...just you.

Now, what to do? ... What to do? Trust this. Time...and the Divine...will lead us.

The Mirror/Distortion Energy

Much of the energy between the Twins can be described as "mirror energy" or even "distortion energy," but "mirror energy" is probably a more simplistic and easier way to describe it.

Let's use the example of organized religion. In a very simplified premise, one could say that organized religion started out with a pure intent. Then, over time, church leaders and other authority figures distorted that energy and started using it for their own purposes and personal gains. Thus, the original intent became distorted. And, then the media (TV, movies, etc.) picked up on that distorted energy and that is what is being (and has been) broadcast out, which has actually hurt organized religion over time, like an eroding shoreline. It was like an authentic thing that turned into some sort of perverse illusion, and then that perverse illusion is what became truth, and that became the truth of today's organized churches and religions (or at least, what many people believe them to be). There was the "real thing" and then there was the "fabricated thing," but the "fabricated thing" became our current reality. Never before in the history of the world has church attendance been so low. That's a whole other book, but my point here is to try to illustrate this metaphor using that example.

The Twins' energy is similar. There is polarity or duality. When you are feeling loving/happy/secure, etc., there's a strong chance that your Twin is holding or experiencing the opposite of those feelings, such as fear/anger/hostility.

There is a simple emotions chart, or wheel that an associate shared with me online (perhaps Google "emotional chart" or "emotional wheel.") This chart was useful in helping me name my emotions (something that most of us, including myself, admittedly, aren't that good at). But it was also a useful tool in seeing how we and our Twins may be mirroring one another. For example, in duality/polarity, the opposite of love on this chart would be fear. You may be in extreme love with your person, and yet, your person may be in fear.

Each person, each counterpart, holds a particular polarity. One is yin, and one is yang. In the middle, there is balance. So, when your Twin is angry or hostile at you, just remember he or she is embodying the opposite side of the wheel. In time, you may, through a great deal of hard work and healing and trial and error, be able to minimize the vast ocean of difference between the two polarities.

The pendulum will swing more to the middle. It's true that nature and the universe always bends toward the middle, toward the neutral ground, toward the zero-point. Eventually.

In the case of me and my Twin, I was in a good space and thought I would check in on her after the harrowing COVID-19 lockdown in the U.S., which turned out (on the surface) to be a stupid thing to do. (I am only joking, as you should always follow your intuition.)

Approaching her with care, concern, and zero expectations, I was met with a string of F-bombs and extreme hostility and a request to never contact her again. Honestly, it was the worst email or communication anyone has ever sent me in my 48 years on this Earth. But I know, deep-down, that deeply wounded people sometimes unintentionally (and sometimes intentionally) harm other people.

Back to my own personal Twin journey, the connection started with pure, unconditional love and pure intention, and through my Twin's distorted lens of things that had happened to her and occurred over her lifetime (and her categorizing or lumping our experience in with those other experiences), my concern and care for her (instead of being met with love, grace, and acceptance) became something worrisome and threatening. The proverbial "monster under the bed." Except … there's no monster. She was essentially projecting all that residual emotional baggage onto me. Because I am a safe target, I suppose.

And Divine Counterpart, if you're reading this now, just know I forgive you, as I always have (and likely, always will). I know you do not ask nor require my forgiveness, but I give it anyway for my own peace of mind. I try not to take any of it personally because I know much of it actually isn't about me. For all of you reading, please reference Don Miguel Ruiz's "The Four Agreements," a book about ancient Toltec wisdom. It's guided the last 20 or so years of my life and it teaches you to never to take anything personally as everyone is playing out their own life story or play and they see with their own lens of perceptions. Perceptions that may sometimes be distorted.

You will find that often, throughout your Journey, others will project their stuff onto you. It's part of the Journey. Our jobs are to transmute all that. To be strong enough to be able to be dumped upon and then to essentially "shake it off." It takes time to do that. It takes practice to do that. Yes, it will most likely happen to you. Yes, it is unpleasant. Sometimes highly so. But it's part of the Journey. To give, to receive, to transmute, to heal. In our healing, we can be that beacon, that single point of light, that lighthouse not just for ourselves, but for others. I've realized I am strong enough to take it and it hurts less and less over time. Yes, it makes me sad, but as they say, "It is what it is." It is part of my own personal Journey, part of my learning process. My process of learning, growing, evolving, thriving. If you don't walk through the valleys, how could you appreciate the summits when you reach them? It's all part of life, all part of our chosen paths.

So, back to the emotional wheel. Check it out. Practice naming your emotions. And then see when and where you and your Twin might have mirrored each other in a very polarizing way, with one of you on one side, and one of you on the extreme opposite of the wheel. I am curious to see if this fits for any of you...? If not, please let me know. But if it does resonate, I'd love to know that, too.

Reflections on this Stage of the Journey

When I wrote *The Twin Flame Guidebook: Your Practical Guide to Navigating the Journey*, I feel I was more like a child, newly initiated into the Twin Flame Journey, enthusiastic, eager, and bright-eyed. Everything about me was flowing (and glowing) with optimism. And that was a very good space to be! I still relish that book and read it frequently from time to time, as a touchstone, as a reminder of all that has transpired so far on my Journey.

Where I am on the Journey now is quite different. It's a matured experience and I am seeing the Journey with new eyes and a new perspective. I remain enthusiastic, but I also remain realistic and practical, as always. (Sometimes I think "practical" is my middle name.)

I've come to realize that as the "chaser" Twin (many people don't like those labels, but I will use it for the purposes of trying to illustrate my point), that I didn't let my Twin "just be." I was so enthusiastic about what I had discovered about Twin Flames (or whatever label you would like to attach to it), about the Journey, about the connection, that I did not let her be in her own space about it all. I was, to be perfectly honest, resistant to her resistance (the mirror!) The more she resisted, though I couldn't help it, the more I pushed. The more I tried to be "right." Though my feelings were all directed by love and enthusiasm and my childlike exuberance, I was in judgment energy, judging that I was what was best for her, and by the way, how couldn't she see that? Right?!? (I write this with no small degree of sarcasm.)

Meanwhile, I've come to recognize that she does know what's best for her and her own Soul Growth, not me. I tried to force it. And she became even more stubborn and resistant. It was like trying to make a window into a door. Trying to just "will it so."

But the truth is, it only pushed her further away, like when you notice a fleck of something in your coffee or your tea, and you try to fish it out, but you can't because it keeps eluding you. Every time you put your finger in, or a spoon, the speck "squeaks by." It squeaks past you, ever-elusive, until you finally give up. It's like that. At this point, there was no understanding on my part. I just couldn't understand it, or process it. There was no grace offered by me.

I could very easily go into beating myself up over all of that, but that wouldn't be productive or helpful. I didn't know what I didn't know. But now I know.

And that's what matters.

So, I have come to recognize a few things. That I am completely okay if this Twin Flame Journey has served its purpose, of awakening me, tossing my world upside down, dumping me and the various components of my life out like a purse or a bag that has been turned over and spilled out everywhere. A time in which I have the opportunity to examine each item in the purse, and to take a close, hard look at it, and decide whether I want to put it back in or not.

So much has changed with me along the way. The things I would have put back in the purse months ago, I may take pause before putting it back in today. And I may not put the thing back in at all.

I compare this to, when I was in my mid to late 20s, I made a very careful, very copious list of all the things I wanted in a partner. It was probably 10 pages long. It was full of many good things, but also several ego-driven items (like occupation, etc.) But the truth was, it was the perfect list for me at that time. Fast forward approximately 20 years later, and I've made yet another list (just to make it for myself). My old list was full of interesting things, but what I believe is that it was mostly focused on superficial things, for the most part. ("I want a partner with a professional job…" "I want a partner with a solid financial foundation…" "I want a partner who says, 'Bless you' when I sneeze…") Yes, I think I got down to that micro level. And the sneezing and good manners part, well, that stands intact. But what changed about the new list I made is that it's just so much more substantial now, and really strikes at the heart of what it means to be a decent, good human. What it means to be someone who has jumped the boundaries of "ordinary" and sees the world with a new and different perspective. Someone not bound by the limitations set forth of the 3-D mindset (birth, school, work, bills, death). Someone who has discovered the meaning of true, unconditional love and who practices that vibration, that frequency, daily. Someone who is introspective, soulful, and led by their heart, not their mind or their ego. (Those two will only get you so far and at times, can even betray you.)

I am not sure that I would want my Twin/Divine Counterpart any longer if she does not resonate with this new space, this new frequency. Though I will always love her and deeply appreciate how she ignited in me this awakening process, the Twin I knew several years ago ... well, I am not sure whether we're in the same vibrational stratosphere, though I do believe many of the good things about her are still true.

Where I stand now, is with my back slightly turned away, and open to all the new possibilities this new stage of the Journey brings. I am no longer looking backward. I may check over my shoulder occasionally, but I am looking forward to the future and I have stepped off the ledge into a vast, new unknown, still led by own bloody, beating heart, but truly led by my own intuition and the nudgings of Source energy. (And if my Twin/Counterpart chooses to meet me here in this new space, well, then, I would welcome her.)

I gave myself over to God/Source energy and asked Him/Her to please allow me to be of service. That purpose unfolds daily, but it feels good. I am feeling my way into the new future. I still don't know where it's taking me (though now as I write this from my hotel room in London, a city I had never before visited), but I know that every day in this new future feels oh-so-much-better than where I was before (both pre-Journey and in many of the Journey's cycles),

when I was buried in doubt, insecurity, sadness, and grief…
all the shadow dust aspects that the Journey "kicks up."

Now, those emotions come into frame less frequently, but
they're still there. But they pass through me far more easily
than before. They're a fleeting notion: they come in, I notice
them, release them, and then they fly on out…to somewhere
else. I don't need those shadow aspects any longer. Previously
I may have clung to them because they were a big part of
what I knew before, but no longer. They only serve to hinder
my self-growth, my self-expansion. And expansion is the
name of this game … always developing, always growing, like
the most beautiful, sprawling aspects of the universe.

I've now come into alignment (if not all the time, well, then,
most of the time). And that feels awesome and fulfilling
and like, finally, at long last, I am on target and on purpose.
Heading for a destination yet unknown with all its raw
potential. That's where you and my Twin will find me.

Connection

As I sit here writing this at home, from my comfy couch spot with my fave gold lamp a'shining beside me and as a global (and national) pandemic rages all around with no foreseeable "wind-down" or end in sight, I've learned something very valuable. I've always known that connection to other human beings is so important. But I never quite realized just how important until I was separated from others in the recommended space or period of "lockdown" because of the COVID-19 pandemic.

"You don't know what you got until it's gone," is a famous line from the Chicago song, "Hard Habit to Break." And it's never been truer for me and so many others as we collectively work through this global challenge (read: opportunity).

The Twin Flame Journey is just that…a connection, a very deep, spiritual connection. It's an expansive connection, a dynamic connection, and an ever-growing connection. This connection is tied to our deepest truths, our deepest unfolding, our deepest karmic lessons, and soul truths. You are deeply connected to your Twin and that is what the Journey is about, but it's also about, and this is perhaps EVEN more important, your connection to your SELF.

You cannot connect deeply to your Twin without first being connected to your Self.

In retreat, or in a separation, or even a heavy separation from your Twin, the learning to look at yourself deeply and connect to yourself deeply is completely meaningful and it's a critical step in the process. Without the (true) connection to Self, your (true) Union could not happen or would not be able to occur in this 3-D world.

So…I challenge you to look at the ways you are disconnected from your Self, or how you deny your connection to your Self. And really be honest about it all.

There are some helpful probing questions you can ask yourself. You may wish to take some time for quiet contemplation or meditation, and you may also wish to journal about this. If you don't know or cannot come up with answers to these questions, talk with a parent (if you have a living parent), if you feel comfortable with that. Or if you don't have a living parent, or you don't feel comfortable asking your parent, then ask a very close friend or your pastor or spiritual advisor, if you have one. (It's very important to always talk with someone you trust.) Another person sometimes can see things about us that we cannot see or understand. You do not have to reveal about your Twin Flame connection, unless you want to and feel comfortable with that, because oftentimes, people who are not on a true Twin Flame Journey cannot begin to understand the dynamics of which you are speaking.

- *What do you want for **you**?*
- *Do you even know what you want for you? Can you articulate it?*

- *What do you want out of life? Can you state that (in a simple statement)?*
- *How or what do you see as your Life Purpose and/or Mission?*
- *How are you blocking yourself from what you want for you and your life?*
- *Are there ways in which you do not support or believe in yourself fully?*
- *Are there ways in which you are self-sabotaging yourself?*
- *Are there ways in which you ever diminished yourself, second-guessed yourself, or times when you let your life or decisions be driven or made based on your Limiting Beliefs*?*
- *Were your Limiting Beliefs ever harmful to you?*

(*Limiting Beliefs are things that you understand, either overtly or covertly, about yourself. It's a way of viewing yourself and your own self-capacity. In this case, these views are generally "negative" – such as "I'm not good enough" or "I'm not worthy." They may be messages you have articulated to yourself or they may never have been articulated to yourself by yourself. BUT...Your beliefs can propel you forward or hold you back like you are being bound or tied or restrained. Limiting Beliefs hold you hostage. They hold you back. They prevent you from doing the types of things or the activities, hobbies, or pursuits you want to do.*)

[*Editor's Note: The author is currently delivering online courses on topics including, but not limited to, Limiting Beliefs and also Connecting to Your Higher Purpose. Please be on the lookout for those on the author's social media and other channels. As soon as it is safe to resume classroom courses, we'll be doing that as well.]

Tools for Your Journey

So, I didn't really realize this consciously when I wrote book one of *The Twin Flame Guidebook: Your Practical Guide to Navigating the Journey*, but it's pretty obvious. (I mean, there's a lot of great content in there, but I missed this obvious thing and I wanted to go back to re-state it a bit more completely, as I've continued to evolve on my own personal Journey.)

1. You're on a Journey. A J-o-u-r-n-e-y. What does a traveler need on a Journey? Well, this means you not only need a traveling companion (one in the 3-D, that is--so if you don't have a good friend to confide in who understands this stuff, then please, do yourself a favor and befriend someone you can trust on Facebook or other online sites, or even maybe someone you meet at your local spiritual store, workshopping event, lecture, etc. Find someone who is in a similar mindset, someone who at the very least understands the concept of soul mates (if not Twin Flames, but ideally, try to find someone who is a Twin Flame). This will be your fellow traveler and many times, your sherpa and your compass, and you may have more than one. (My traveling companion knows who she is ... and my "tribe" of gals know who

they are. Thank you to all of them. I couldn't be doing this without you.) For you, your person or group of people will be your support group to keep you safe and sane as you go about this process of awakening (which includes a whole bunch of steps I am not going to get into here, for purposes of brevity). They will help you understand your Journey, provide context, and help you see that you are not alone as this process unfolds for you. You'll also see and hear many commonalities that will provide you with the reassurance you are seeking and that you need.

2. You need some tools for your Journey. Like, start with the following two. There may be more, but these are the ones I know of so far that have been indispensable to me on my path.

    a. **Experienced local and/or YouTube tarot card reader** - On our Journey (or at least mine), I would have been lost without at least the annual guidance of my fave local tarot card reader, who not only is a great technical reader of the cards for me, but she is also an intuitive, so she can add a great deal more context and insight to the spreads she pulls for me. I took notes from those sessions and those have been valuable touchstones to refer back to as I have gone about this process of unfolding and evolving over a couple of years now. Maybe ask around or look online for a reader who has strong reviews or comes from a place that is highly recommended online. There are many folks out there reading the cards, but believe you me, they aren't created equally and some are far better than the others. (And beware, some will just downright try to "scam" you. While these "bad apples" are few and far between, please be wary, and use your discernment and intuition to choose the right reader for you.)

If you don't have, or can't find a good one locally, then I also highly recommend listening to readers like Sylvia Escalante [formerly Twin Flame Enchantress and now known as "The Enchanted World of Twin Flame(s)"]; Aqua Moonlight; Elizabeth Grove (Paranormal Priestess); K Moon; Lee and Sherry Patterson (a Twin Flame couple in Union at Relationship Reinvented); Twinfinity (also a Twin couple in Union), and WaterBaby Tarot by Bomispirit. These knowledgeable, intuitive, and insightful people are probably my top readers/channelers/resources who resonate the most for me. It doesn't mean that others aren't great...these are just my usual "go-to's." Several of them help read for the energy of the Divine Feminine and the Divine Masculine Collectives (and most of them offer private readings and helpful sessions, as well).

b. **A pendulum** - The second thing that I recommend you get (stat!) if you don't have one is a pendulum. I figured out this tool completely by accident. A good friend of one of my kids gave me a pendulum, kind of out of the blue, but following after some somewhat spiritual discussions that we had. She is a like-minded gal and she thought I needed one, based on what I was sharing. I just bought one for my Twin Flame companion on this Journey (not my Twin, but we are like Sister Twins, or soul flames or something like that) for $12 at my local spiritual store. A pendulum is a simple divination tool that will answer "yes" or "no" to your questions. It cannot get into long esoteric conversations, but it can give you insight and point you in a particular direction (or not!) and it can also confirm your intuitions and things you are thinking or feeling about your personal development, about your Twin Flame, or about your Journey. There are good videos online on YouTube that show you simply and quickly how to use this tool that has become invaluable on my Journey (and to many people I know who are also on the Journey).

With these simple and highly effective "tools," you'll be able to remain centered, stable, safe, and sane as you traverse the twisty, turny Twin Flame path.

Don't Over-Rely on Your 3-D Senses

One of the things I intuitively knew all along my Journey was that my heart, my intuition, could be trusted. I will say my Twin, a Divine Masculine, kind of went the opposite way, putting all her faith into logic and thinking with her head. She tried to reason this all away because it didn't make sense. I was led completely by my own bloody, beating heart that always "led first."

In this Journey, you'll need to "dial back" your 3-D orientation and go more with "feeling into it." You'll need to "feel your way" into people, situations, and how things really, truly are. Don't fall into the 3-D trap of sharing this approach, as people (particularly those online) will be brutal and tell you you're a "stalker," "you have a bad case of wishful thinking," "you're [crazy], [delusional], a [nut job], [mental]." It could be any of these adjectives, or all of them at once. That's why the first rule of Twin Flame (like "Fight Club") is don't talk about Twin Flame. Not with anyone who is not a true Twin. If you can avoid it. They just won't understand. They can't. The material, the information, the content, isn't FOR them.

This new way of thinking and approaching life will not make sense. It will feel almost like defying the laws of gravity, but that's kind of what you are doing. The higher 5-D spiritual "laws" are completely different than what is presented here in this earthly landscape. The truth is the truth is the truth, even though at times everything and everyone in the 3-D will try to fight and resist it. They'll even try to twist it. They're twisting it. Not you. Not if your intuition tells you something. Trust that. Go with that. Always. It will never lead you wrong. (Unless of course, your mind or that inner voice is telling you to do something unlawful or unethical. That is NOT the voice of good. So, don't listen to that. You'll be able to discern good and pure versus not-so-good and impure.) As you go along your Journey, you'll get better and better at this. Trust me.

"Feeling into it"…it's a feeling. It's not thinking. Turn your brain off. Let your heart speak. Your heart knows what it wants. Your heart also knows the truth of your connection in ways you cannot understand. Don't question it. Don't undermine it. Don't try to explain it away.

Standing in Your Truth

Blasted Out of the Bunker

So, in my Journey, I had carefully constructed things in a way so that everything was neat and compartmentalized (or so I thought). I had come out of my "spiritual closet" a bit, but I was still "in hiding" from my karmic and from my Twin (in certain ways, though I might have preferred to be a little less "in hiding with her," in all truth). I had quietly written a little book under my pen name called *"The Twin Flame Guidebook"* (the first book) and I had quietly placed it at a couple of retail locations around my town and on Amazon, on Barnes & Noble, and on Ingram (one of the leading national wholesalers for all books being released in the U.S., and later with Gardners in the UK). I had kept all my writing, editing, and publishing activities, both on and off the web, under wraps, or so I thought. I had one foot on the shoreline, one food in the water. I thought I had it all balanced. But again, not so fast, said the Universe/Source Energy.

It had other plans.

My karmic partner somehow, someway, found my blogs on Quora (of course, written under my pen name to "protect" everyone) and she also found a video that one of my creative partners had done referencing my real first name. And the rest of this is a bit fuzzy, but I will capture and explain it to the best of my understanding. I do not know how, where, or why my karmic came to know of the Quora blog series (about Twin Flames, naturally). As I understand it, my karmic partner then decided to send a link of one of them to my Twin, as we had all known each other prior to everything going "south" and had the personal connection and contact information to be able to do that. (Either my karmic or someone else did, but I don't know for sure.)

It seemed, somehow, from my Twin's response, that (possibly) my Twin also knew of the blogs (and possibly the book), all at the same time, all right before a major holiday that shall remain unidentified (to protect the identity of the holiday)... ha ha...just a little levity to keep this somewhat light.

At any rate, I had tried to do what I needed to do to document this journey in an effort to capture it and a way to begin to hope to understand it (and maybe, just maybe, helping others along the way), but also to conceal and hopefully protect my family situation (particularly my kids), my identity, and my truth.

But it was as if the Universe/Source threw a hand grenade right into my self-constructed bunker and destroyed it, so I was left standing, naked, for the whole world to see (and read).

That's truly what it felt like. So I had my Twin on the one side lobbing more written grenades at me in the form of text messages that could be categorized as somewhat threatening and I had my karmic on the other side reading whole passages of my book to me out loud while I was trapped in the car with her alone whilst in another state on a long-planned family vacation (*that* was fun).

That's about as far as I will go into *that*, but what did being blasted out of my bunker teach me? It taught me that Universe/Source energy will do what it needs to do to get you to be authentic and to stand in your truth. Because if you avoid it...or worse, you lie, it only gets worse from there. The best and only way out of it, is to tell the truth, every time, to the extent you can (without harming yourself or another, or others). The lesson is: stand up, be authentic, be true, be counted. Speak your truth. Even though it can be uncomfortable beyond belief, you may just feel liberated when it's all said and done.

Eventually, I was like (maybe not the exact words, but the sentiment) "Yeah, that's that. And that's how it is." At a certain point, my karmic had also asked me to renounce my Twin, renounce the experience, to take it all back. The truth is, I would rather die than renounce my Twin and the Journey. That would be like me refuting the Divine, refuting miracles. Over time, everyone involved just had to deal with the situation and circumstances, and believe me, I know it was hugely uncomfortable for all involved, to say the least, though I don't have a lot of details of how it felt or was experienced from their perspectives. Of course, I felt (and feel) badly for hurting others (when the truth did hurt others), but dammit, it's my truth, it's my perspective, it's my experience, and I am entitled to it.

In one of the other chapters of this book, I repeated a line I love from a George Michael song, "Father Figure," where he writes and croons so aptly that "sometimes love can be mistaken for a crime." It would seem that, to tell the world you love someone wouldn't be a bad thing, a negative thing. It would seem also that your karmic partner would be glad to know exactly what *is* going on inside that head of yours (especially if you've been holding many of your "true" feelings in). I admit. It **was** liberating, even though it wasn't voluntary. It was truly a relief when it all came out. And it couldn't have tumbled out more "cleanly" or more "finally" than it did. And granted, it wasn't comfortable and hasn't been since, but it's my truth and I am living it, and it's better all out in the open than boxed up inside somewhere, where it will never—and would never—see the light of day. Yes, I do continue to write with my pen name for a couple of reasons, but perhaps most important of all, because my son has asked me to.

You see, I still love my Twin, no matter how she feels for me. It's just that plain and simple. I can't imagine anything in the world would ever change that. I don't require anything of her, though, and I have no hidden agendas, and I'm not sorry for ultimately sharing what is on my heart for her. I'm not sorry for the experience of being a Twin Flame or for being on the Journey. I'll never be sorry about my Twin, the feelings I have (or have had) for her, the great friends I've made along the way, the travels all over, the mission work I've been able to perform and complete through *The Twin Flame Guidebook*, the self-love and respect I've discovered, the people I've been able to help, the joy of living out my life purpose and following my destined path. So, thank you, Universe. Thank you, Source Energy. You've broken me down and built me back up again in the most delicious, most rewarding of ways. And for that I am eternally grateful. May I always be worthy.

Integrity

No matter what happens on your Journey, along the way, try to be as authentic and as honest and as transparent as possible (within reason). Our spiritual Journeys and paths require it of us, but there are times and reasons when you will not be able to be as fully authentic, honest, and transparent as you'll want to be (at times, this will be to protect others or to protect your family unit or your partner).

The only thing you can do when karmic cycles are completing, and karmic lessons being learned, is to stand in your authority and tell your truth. This, truth, is a 4-D orientation and as you know, we are moving more and more into a higher dimensional state of being. At times, it may be uncomfortable. At times, it may hurt so see or experience the hurt of others. If you're empathic like me, you will feel their hurt and it will hurt you, too.

For a while in my Journey, I was hiding out until the Universe decided it would not be so any longer. The Universe decided to reveal my book and that I was its author at the exact same time (seemingly) to both my karmic partner of 20 years and to my Divine Counterpart. I thought it would be a safer route to write under the pen name. Also, my son had asked that for any spiritual books I would write, to please put them under a pen name. He did not want to be embarrassed (which I understood), with him being a teenage boy.

But, as Fate would have it, and as the Divine would have it…they gave me a chance to come fully clean many times. I did not. (This may be the lesson for you, as well, as it will all come out eventually.) The Universe and Source Energy was requiring me to be honest and speak my truth. At times, I did not. Until honestly, Universe/Source Energy made me do it by an unfolding series of events, as I've described. I've heard and read that along the way…that if you don't deal with something, it only gets bigger and hairier to deal with, and if you keep putting it off, well, then, the Universe/Source will find a way to make it come out anyway. And it may be louder and even more uncomfortable when it finally does come out. I am not sure why it works that way, but that is the way it worked for me, validating all those things I'd read and heard over the course of many years.

So, here I am, dealing with the aftermath. There was no other option than to tell the whole truth, the full truth, and nothing but the truth to both my karmic partner and my Divine Counterpart. It was really messy at times and very uncomfortable at times. It's true that there's still fallout, but my karmic partner is handling it better than I ever thought, though I cannot know whether my Divine Counterpart deeply hates me or loves me (due to Separation). This requires blind faith, as I said, and the truth is, it would hurt me deeply if my Divine Counterpart does not ever return or reciprocate my feelings, but that may be the way it's meant to be, and if that is the case…then I must acknowledge that my Twin and I designed it that way, prior to incarnation on Earth, and the focus was to be on the karmic lessons I learned along the way and the tests of honesty, integrity, and patience that I hopefully passed with flying colors. That's all I can know… that's all I can see. And that is what I have to accept, and what I do accept. Let the chips fall where they may. I did all I could do. I showed up. I felt and expressed unconditional love. I held that space for my Twin. I loved her unconditionally all this time, and I still do. And the truth is, I always will.

The Deep and Undeniable Communication Connection With Your Twin

I wrote in Book One of *The Twin Flame Guidebook: Your Practical Guide to Navigating the Journey* about telepathy with your Twin and how it's not just possible, but probable, and downright real. Many Twins in Union have confirmed that they experience regular, frequent telepathy with their Twin. It goes far beyond coincidence. It goes far beyond just "knowing your partner well" (like an old married couple would know one another). It's knowing one another's thoughts, feelings, and indeed, even their words, before they speak them.

Yes, Twin Flame telepathy *is* real and it often happens across what I consider to be the 5-D realms, but it also goes far beyond that.

Many Twins that I have talked with (and indeed I have, as well) have experienced the sensation of having a real-life conversation with your Twin that is beyond the words exchanged. It's like, say for example, you spend an hour with your Twin, and it feels timeless: Your mind is thinking and hanging on every word they are saying, and time passes so quickly. But even beyond the words you exchanged during your time together, you covered so much more ground in your communications, in your energy fields (that were also communicating and conversing while you were together).

Another way to state this is that when Twins are together, it's like the communication is so much deeper than the actual words being spoken. For example, spending say, four hours with them, you cover so much verbal/emotional/spiritual territory, that it would be difficult to type up notes from that because everything in THEM is communicating to EVERYTHING in YOU.

When you speak/interact, you are not only talking in the verbal sense, but your energy fields are also talking. They are saying to one another: "Are we in vibrational alignment?" They are sensing or feeling into that.

Your bodies are signaling things to the other as well. You'll notice if he or she is trying to maintain a "respectable distance" or if he or she moves their chair ever so much closer to you.

Your emotions are signaling valuable things to you as well, such as how you're feeling. You'll probably have an ecstatic high from interacting with him or her. This can go on for hours or days after. Your heart will be receiving their heart's signal and your own heart will be broadcasting to him or her your very own signal.

Or, this phenomenon can be illustrated if you write your Twin a letter or an email. You'll write a sentence or a paragraph, and the words can sometimes be like poetry, with meanings behind the stated meanings, going far deeper than surface-level. It's truly a communications exchange on a whole different level, and it is unparalleled, in my experience. Which is basically me saying that I've never had that experience before, with another person, in my life.

Dealing With Separation

"Delusional"

Many of you on this Journey *may* be called "crazy" or "delusional" along the way, by your Twin, by your "friends," or by others. That's okay and honestly, completely normal.

That's because we are shattering the old paradigms of love and relationships and honestly, the 3-D world just does not know how to classify what you are feeling, experiencing, and communicating. Once you start being honest and transparent and sharing how you feel, the truth is, it's going to open you up to this type of false classification. The catchall bucket that society will generally try to use for anything beyond their understanding, for anything beyond their reach, beyond their ability to categorize and compartmentalize is "crazy" or "delusional."

I can list about a million things in this world that are "crazy," but true, unconditional love isn't one of them. At the risk of getting too political, caging humans at the U.S. Southern border with no plan or policy for their release is crazy. The top 1 percent hoarding money and resources while the other 99 percent are left to fight and scramble for food, housing, jobs, resources, health care...*that's* crazy. But I digress and don't wish to get too political within these pages, though it would be easy for me to do.

Of course, hearing such loaded words as "delusional" or "crazy" from anyone you care about or love can be very hurtful to hear and to sort out, and it can make you angry and sad, but again, it's all part of the process of you shedding the old "you." Shedding the old convictions and belief systems.

Just think of all the great people in history who were called crazy...the rebels, the dreamers, the artists, the visionaries, the religious leaders. Jesus. Da Vinci. Joan of Arc. Isaac Newton. Van Gogh. Albert Einstein. Nikola Tesla. Winston Churchill. John Lennon. Gandhi. If you think they fit in, well, they didn't. They were the square pegs in the round holes.

When people try to categorize you in this way, it's only part and parcel of them trying to understand something new and very foreign to them because everything in them is conditioned this way. Most conditioned minds—most of them—cannot begin to understand love without expectation, love without reward. Which in many cases, *is* the Twin Flame Journey.

Would I choose being "crazy" or "delusional"...would I practically die trying to bring a new template of unconditional love to this planet? I would. I would pick being "crazy" and "delusional" any day over not trying to leave this planet better than I found it.

If you're on this Journey, you have the wisdom of the Ancients at your disposal. You are unleashed from the parameters and the constrictions of the ordinary, 3-D world. Your life is no longer linear. It can be circular, trapezoidal, heart-shaped, or whatever shape you choose to make it. It is *whatever* you choose to make it. And NOTHING that anyone can say, nor any of their words, can lessen or diminish you. Most of our mothers and fathers always told us this as we grew up, but a person's words are often more about *them* and their fears or projections than they are about you. For some powerful help with this subject, I would like to refer you again to Don Miguel Ruiz's excellent book, "The Four Agreements," based on ancient Toltec wisdom that has guided the last 20 years or so of my life. One of the agreements is to "Take nothing personally." A person's words about you are more about their projection or perception of the world and their own life experience than they are about you as an individual.

And truly, also, as the schoolyard taught: "Sticks and stones may break my bones, but words will never hurt me." I'm not trying to dismiss the hurtful nature of anything your Twin has ever (or may ever) say to you. Yes, it hurts. It cuts deeply, but let those words wash over you and through you. Let them pass right through you. Don't hold on to them. You are your own person with your own unique and valuable perspectives. You've got your own reality to create, and you do, every day. Yes, the words may temporarily shake you or make you take pause, but don't let them put you in to a downward spiral, because then you're giving over your power to another person's words. Stand in your own knowing, stand in your own authority, stand in your sovereignty, and stand in self-love for yourself. You are more powerful than you know.

No Contact

As I mentioned, there's that famous, wonderful line from a beautiful George Michael song, "Father Figure." It goes: "Sometimes love can be mistaken for a crime."

You may feel this way, particularly if you've been blocked by your Twin Flame on social media (or elsewhere), or if he or she has requested "no contact."

Maybe you were even flying high in the connection, even in the 3-D. Maybe you had some great outings or conversations. Then, something happened and you triggered one another again, resulting in Separation.

The blocking and "no contact" request that sometimes follows is perhaps the most hurtful, deepest, darkest part of the Journey. Immediately, we are thrown back into the "Dark Night of the Soul" (in my case, a place and mind-space I thought I was done with, having experienced it several times before).

If you've received a "no contact" request, or have been blocked, now is honestly not the time to push the connection further or to inquire further. Now is the time for us to move our mental energy and attention elsewhere, to go inward again, to go deep again. To talk to friends again, ones who understand. To find—and to connect with—our tribe(s). To work on surfacing, realizing, acknowledging, healing and purging core wounds that we have around rejection, self-worth, and abandonment.

It is a great time to figure out what you DO want in a connection, in a relationship, whether with your Twin or someone else. And what you want from life.

As for me, I know I choose happiness.

I choose health and wellness.

I choose wholeness.

I choose to surround myself with people who feel like sunshine.

Sometimes your Twin will block you without communicating why. Sometimes they "use their words."

In my case, my Twin's words, which were very hurtful, do not (and did not) define me or who I am. Coming from your Twin, hurtful words can be the most devastating you can hear from anyone in your entire lifetime.

It felt (and sometimes feels, still) like her intent was that of the dragons of Games of Throne, to set fire to me, to scorch the Earth like the dragons scorched King's Landing until there was nothing left, no walking human in sight, the majestic buildings destroyed to burning embers.

But, even though she is my Twin, she should know, nonetheless, I will rise, if not like a Nightwalker, then like the Phoenix, right out of the ashes. I will rise into a stronger and better version of myself than before. Every time I get knocked down, it makes me stronger. Truly, I no longer need, nor require, her validation.

Now is the time for you, for all of us, to be authentic and to speak and stand in our truth. We shouldn't shy away from that. But we do need to detach and stop chasing in the 3-D and even energetically. Shifting your mental energy away is like having the TV on in the background (it's always "on"), but you're not tuning in to the show. Though you won't be giving up on unconditional love, it's time to take a step back and see what happens and what unfolds. And trust me, it will require patient endurance.

If I knew someone loved me this much, I think, I HOPE, I would embrace it. Truly, it's the dream everyone has: to be loved unconditionally.

However, I can accept if she will never choose me. It's possible she may not, in this lifetime, or in future ones. I cannot force it. I cannot force her hand even though I know what is true, that we are divinely connected, and nothing can ever sever the connection. To the 3-D mindset, that may be considered "crazy" and "delusional."

But that is where we are.

But I must wonder, why do I have the fierce devotion, and she is so ready to cast me aside, to deny me and the connection...over and over again? What dynamic is this? It cuts deeply, but each time something like this happens (over the course of roughly three-and-a-half years), I find it actually hurts less than it used to, because I now understand the dynamic and what is going on.

In the 3-D world, these words—the words of "no contact" would be "it." It would mean forever and ever. But we're on a different Journey now, a spiritual journey with a different timeline, a time and space with different dynamics than we are used to.

Based on past experience, it is a possibility that she will be "back." But it could take months or years. I know that now. I know my job now is to send her love and forgiveness, but also to keep loving and forgiving myself, to keep investing in myself, and to follow my mission and soul purpose. There's nothing else to be done. There's nothing else to do.

I will back off, let things do their work. Let the thing manifest...or not. It's time for us to trust the Universe and to trust Source Energy and face the fact that perhaps the Universe has greater things in store for us than even we can know or realize.

We can drive ourselves crazy wondering if our Twins saw something we posted, or if they read something we wrote. Trust me, I did drive myself crazy with a million questions and it's an unnecessary distraction when you think about it. Chances are, our Twins probably did read or look at the things we wondered about.

Our job, then, now is to continue loving our Twins with consistency and constancy, but most important, to start (or keep) loving ourselves. And in finding that deep love for ourselves, we will have won not only ourselves, but the equivalent of the entire world. No one, nor anything, can ever take that away from us, no matter what transpires.

Dark Night of the Soul (Part II)

In *The Twin Flame Guidebook: Your Practical Guide to Navigating the Journey* (Book One), I included a simple process map so that you can visualize the different stages of the Twin Flame Journey.

The truth is, throughout your Journey, you may not endure the Dark Night of the Soul only once, but many times. The good news is, while this step can be very devastating and some of the lowest emotions that you can (or will) ever experience, it gets a little easier to endure each time.

What is the Dark Night of the Soul (also abbreviated as DNOTS)?

This is the point in time where your Beloved has either rejected you, denied you, or separated himself or herself from you. It can also follow blocking on social media and "no contact" requests. It can also follow your Twin getting together with someone else (and in TwinFlameLandia, this is usually called a "third party.") This is the period of time in which you will languish in despair and you may find yourself down on your knees praying to God or Source energy for help and guidance. You will find yourself missing your Twin more than you ever thought possible. This time period will be when you experience the lowest lows of your life, and you'll be caught or stuck in a seeming "bottomless" pit of low-vibrational emotions (sadness, anger, doubt, fear, jealousy, resentment). You may find yourself questioning "Why me?" or "Why this?" or "What now?" It will feel as if every last ounce of hope has left your body and that going on without your Beloved in your 3-D life is pointless. You will feel hopeless and more heartbroken than you have perhaps ever felt in your entire life.

What's the cure for these feelings and this process? The best answer I have come up with is time, and working on yourself. Working to heal the parts of you that you feel this Journey has ripped wide open, like a wound. How does one work through this all, and "do the work," as we say? It starts with the unconscious things becoming conscious. Things will occur to you in broad daylight (reasons why certain things happened, reasons why you or your Twin acted the way they did), or concepts or suggestions will come to you in the dreamspace. Identify the issue or the patterns, and then work to heal it. This will help take you toward the path of Ascension, where Soul Growth becomes (or will become) your number one priority.

Time in nature can help heal you, as well, because in nature, you see the beauty and perfection of everything, just as it is. You see that nothing in nature is wasted, and as I've said, the same goes for love. Your love is **never wasted**.

So, just know, that your first Dark Night of the Soul will come and go. Your second DNOTS will also come and go, and so on and so on. It really does get easier each time, until you reach the point of surrender and going with the flow and you reach a place of peace, balance, and harmony, as you await whatever great thing the Divine is taking you to next.

Free Will

Free will. It's a thing. A very real thing. In fact, it's a Universal Law and it is a dynamic of this Journey that is a very central component for both (if not, all) parties.

It's important to recognize that your Divine Counterpart has free will and has every right to exercise it, as do you.

What I recognized as part of my Journey and as part of my "chaser" persona (and what I later realized on the flipside for my Divine Counterpart) is that conquest has long been part of our approach to love and relationships. Instead of relaxing and allowing love to come in and take over, many of us have relied on the conquest of others in order to realize and fulfill our physical and emotional desires and to direct relationships in the way we wish them to go. People (er, persons), rather than being seen as divine, sovereign beings, are often seen as the objects of our desire and affection and many of us have sought to push ourselves and our will onto others to fulfill our own (sometimes selfish) needs.

In the past, in the regular, 3-D world, this has largely worked for me (and I dare say, for many of us). And I think it's worked for my Twin, when she wanted to exercise her "powers" in that area. But, in the Twin Flame Journey, that desire to control and the effort to control just does not work because it isn't the natural state of things or the natural state of divine love. It's not about power and control. It's not about manipulation. It's not about domination. It's not about pushing your will or your desires onto another.

It's not about controlling another or being more "powerful" than another. It's truly about unconditional love, love with ZERO conditions. It is your duty (and honor) to love even if the love is not reciprocated, even if the person chooses not to be with you. You both have come into this Twin Flame Journey as divine, sovereign beings with your independence and free will.

That is why your efforts on the Journey, if driven by the mind and ego, if driven to fulfill your own self-purposes, will fail every time. That is why things will not go as you wish. Because you are not in alignment with the Divine Mind and Divine Will. Divine Mind/Divine Will respects the sovereignty of the individual. Both parties have to come to this partnership equally and willingly. And if one of the two does not, then, that person has the right to exercise their free will. It is our job to respect their wishes, and to respect their boundaries, whatever those boundaries are.

Trust me, I got this wrong...a LOT. In fact, I feel as if I've made every "mistake" in the book along the way. But truly, there are no mistakes in this. Only lessons and opportunities. And the discomfort you will encounter along the way is actually good because it pushes you beyond your comfort zone and far beyond familiar terrain, and that's where the learning lies. The truth was, I was so overcome with the concept of Twin Flame and I am such a romantic that I threw myself into this Journey, into this connection, 100 percent. My sense was, if you meet the person you've dreamed of, and you sense and feel the soul connection, then you should pursue it with your entire being and your whole heart and soul. Surely, if you incarnated together in this lifetime, I felt, there was a reason for that. And that last part is true: You *should* pursue it with all your being; however, if the other person isn't feeling it, then it's your responsibility to back off and let the Divine take over. That's where I tried to insert my own free will and it was like standing up in the middle of a raging river against the current. Trust me: *That* will wear you out. You cannot direct this Journey. You just can't. If you try, it will break you. I'm not kidding.

Unconditional love means you love the other person unconditionally. Even if they don't love you back, in the same way. You may feel as if this is some sort of tragedy...all this extreme love, and no place to put it (though you can and should give that love back to yourself). But it's important to remember, for you to love with this degree of passion, with this degree of certainty, you are still VICTORIOUS in that love. Because how many people in life get to experience true, unconditional love for another? Mind-blowing, powerful, earth-shattering love? Not that many. Trust me, in time, you'll see that it's all worth it, no matter how it shakes out for you in the 3-D.

One of the most important things to remember: This Twin Flame Journey is not a romantic Journey. It is primarily a spiritual one, though it does work out for some people to be together romantically and physically in this lifetime, in their current 3-D incarnation. Though romance and physicality and 3-D confirmation would likely be embraced by most (if not all of us), this Journey is not necessarily *that*. But, it will be for some of you. So, hang tight, dear, and do not lose heart. In nature, God wastes nothing, and your love is not wasted; it will never be wasted.

(No) Guarantees

In all my readings on Quora, in various Facebook Groups, in YouTube, in so many forums online (and in the minds of Twin Flames everywhere) lies the timeless and nagging question: "Will my Twin and I enter into Divine Union, together?" (Or some variation of that question). Where, when, how … you name it … there's a question about it and nearly everyone has that question.

The honest truth is, we just don't know whether we and our Twin will come into Union in this lifetime, and just like all things in life, there is no guarantee. It is entirely dependent on a multitude of factors: Free will (both you and your Twin); karmic factors; the soul lessons you and your Twin signed up for, before incarnation, and last, but not least, the willingness and ability to "do the work." And by doing the work, meaning acknowledging the triggers that make you go "cray-cray" and working through them with whatever healing modality you might choose, whether it's talking to a friend, therapy, energy healing such as Reiki, journaling (and many more). There are literally as many ways to heal as there are ways of getting hurt. "The work" means making the subconscious conscious (or once the subconscious thought or "Limiting Belief" floats to the surface), acknowledging it, purging it, healing it, and moving on.

There is also no guarantee that your Twin won't hurt you or be cruel to you. There's not. That may indeed happen, and it doesn't mean that "you're karmics" to each other, and it doesn't mean you are accepting a toxic relationship. If you are a true Twin, the Journey has its ups and downs. Twins are designed to trigger one another, and that can come in a variety of ways.

Most Twins are very strong-minded, and some (not all) can be stubborn or very stubborn. I would place my Twin and me in the "very stubborn" category, without a doubt. I have some Twin friends who just are not willing to do the work and that is okay. It's their choice. Free will, as I've said, is a very real thing. Maybe it's just not time yet. And time. Let's talk about that for a minute. Nothing happens before its time. Divine Timing is a very real factor and a very real phenomenon. And, Divine Timing doesn't move or flow in the way our conception of time works. In the Higher Realms, "time" can take a lot longer than our conception of 3-D "time." To the Heavens, "soon," could mean a long, long time from now. But before you get discouraged, I also acknowledge that, "If God wills it, it will be so." I do believe Divine Will trumps all will, including free will. Now, many people will not like me saying that and many will argue. That's ok.

Many Twins in Union say that even despite their protests, it was clear that God was going to bring them together, no matter what. The Western astrologer and Twin Flame intuitive K. Moon has several good videos available on

YouTube of Twins in Union, and I cannot recommend those videos highly enough, as they showcase or portray real Twins telling their real-life stories, their struggles, and their victories, and all the miraculous things that happened as they were traversing the Journey and the path to Union. There are many tales of people coming together in Union despite (seemingly) impossible odds. It's all possible. Anything is possible. Don't lose sight of that.

Another Love Letter to My Twin

My dearest Twin Flame/Divine Counterpart/Ascension Partner,

This is an honest love letter to you from me. It won't feel like a "love" letter by what I am going to say to you, but it needs to be said (though you may never read this, or hear it). Indeed, you most likely won't be open to hearing it. But yes, I love you. I love you unconditionally. And yet, you've never been able to return or reciprocate that love back. Why is that? I've searched myself. Now I ask you to search yourself and be honest with yourself. I hope if someone loved me as much as I do you, that I would embrace that. But I just don't...and won't...know because the roles are reversed.

I've loved you for almost three-and-a-half years (and some would say, for an eternity), for I know that past lives are real.

I do know you have carried, both in this life, and the ones prior, great burdens and faced and overcome great challenges. You've had tremendous successes, too. In all the roles we served and played, you were a warrior, you were a priestess, you were a maiden, you were a wife, you were a mother, you were a daughter, you were a husband, and you played your roles so well. All I know is I have known you before. And I know, beyond the shadow of a doubt, that you have known me.

When you turned me away, denied me, five times now, I took my lumps, as they say. Each time, your rejection of me got progressively easier until I had healed my issues of not only rejection, but abandonment and lack of self-worth. I returned to my own well time and again, and I worked it. I dug deep, and I worked on it, on me, until my hands were bloody and bruised. Now I stand strong, in my sovereignty, in my power. And I tell you, though I still love you and would do practically anything for you, I will never, ever compromise myself again. I will not allow you to dance all over me and my boundaries, to stomp on me like a useless weed, to hurl angry and harmful descriptions and insults at me, as if I am not a human and have no feelings, and no ability to feel.

You've called me "delusional." What's delusional is accepting this world as it is, and being okay with it. What's delusional is accepting fake love and substituting it for real, authentic love (or even settling for lesser loves) because we…our or society…cannot even recognize or accept real, true love for what it is. Our views and our perceptions of love have become so distorted, that we think it is unattainable or something only for fairytales and romance novels. You, my counterpart, view love through society's eyes. You view relationships through society's eyes. You view your potential partners through society's eyes. You view love through ego's eyes. Not your own. You view connection as a threat, like a foreign invader, a virus, to be conquered. And I know, because I can feel your energy (as you feel mine) that anxiety regularly and frequently eats you up, from the inside out. Could you for once, try following the true inclinations of your own heart? Can you even feel your heart (versus your head)? Can you sense where your own heart is trying to lead you? Do you even know what your own heart truly desires? Have you ever dared to write it down? Not the superficial truths, but the real, authentic ones? The ones you are *afraid* to write down?

I can tell you, I have never, and will never, talk to another human being as you have talked to me. I will never, ever treat another human being as you have treated me. But I know that wounded people sometimes hurt other people (sometimes covertly, sometimes overtly), and so for that, I offer you my forgiveness. I know you do not seek nor need my forgiveness, but still, I offer it to you so that *my* soul may have peace. And I shall not drink the poison of unforgiveness, nor allow it to harden my heart or my soul. I do not need, nor crave, your validation, because I've already found that within myself.

Perhaps you think I see you as weak? I don't. I never have. You are stronger than even *you* know. But how do I know, deep-down, that **you** see **yourself** as weak? Because of the way you've responded to me defensively in the past, time and again. And because truly strong people never have to belittle or be mean to other people. You're not weak, but you've bought into the illusion that you are, by your past experience, by your past choices, by your past relationships. But that's not who you are at your core. You're more powerful than can be measured. You're only limited by your own beliefs. And you feel restless and you feel trapped, but only you have the power to set yourself free, not me.

You've spent so long looking and longing for the ordinary, the ordinary relationship, that you missed it when the extraordinary came calling upon your door. Yes, that's right. You missed it. Because you were focused elsewhere. That's sad to me, and I hope you see the reality of this statement someday.

I want you to know I see you and I know you in ways that cannot be explained by earthly explanations. I see how I pushed you too hard as I was so excited about discovering this connection and all its dynamics and I was compelled by the mystical pull of it all. I pushed you too hard for that reason, but in the light of these new days, I can not only SEE, but FEEL and EXPERIENCE how uncomfortable that made you feel, for whatever reasons, and for that, I am truly sorry. I hope you understand my viewpoint, my experience, and my perspective at some point in the future and respect them, as I do you and yours.

I love you and I know we could feel, achieve, and do great things together (and I truly know in my heart of hearts, that we are better together than apart) as I have seen your true heart, your true being, and your true nature in the higher realms (you're beautiful in every way there), but I have surrendered it all over to Divine Will and Divine Timing. I know that I cannot know what is best for you. I may not even truly know what is best for me because I tend to pick the wounded. I tend to pick the emotionally unavailable, and I tend to pick the struggling (or at least, that's been my pattern). I know that only God knows what is best for each of us. So, I release you to God, to your world, to your activities, to the busy-ness you have constructed, to your seeming desire to feed and indulge your ego continuously. I release you to your path, to your sovereignty, to whatever it is that you may choose, for free will is a very real thing. It's a Universal Law.

You say you don't believe in all this (or any of this), and of course, you have that right. Please know: You are not beholden to me, nor my beliefs. I do not hold you as beholden to me. I honestly and completely release you and surrender to Divine Will.

Though I've known you forever, in this lifetime, I don't presume to know you really at all, because you have hidden yourself from me, time and again. It's unfortunate that you were not able or willing to give this love, this pure, Divine Love, a chance. For it is true, it is real, it is lasting, and it is forever. I do wish you well, with all the love I have in my heart. Only time ... and lifetimes ... and other timelines ... will tell.

Godspeed.

"He's/She's Not Doing Their 'Fair Share' of the Work"

If you're reading this and you are upset or angry or even resentful that your Twin isn't doing his or her part toward making your Union happen, then it's time for us to take a look at that. I am talking predominantly here about Divine Masculines (DMs), but this can apply to Divine Feminines (DFs), as well.

Last night, I received a very clear message from my guides that in most cases, our DMs really got the crappy end of the stick when it came/comes to their 3-D lives.

In my own relationship (or connection) to my DM, I had never really thought about this too much because she had never really opened up about her past or what had happened in her life and relationships. For the most part, up until only recently, she kept most everything on lockdown, very close to her chest and when sensitive topics would come up in discussion, she would shut them down or end them very quickly. So, there was a whole mountain of stuff that I just never knew about until my guides brought the understanding in to me that she has had a somewhat difficult or challenging life, in certain ways, and the things that have happened to her have been very painful. Not much more than that was revealed, but as it was "coming in to me," I felt a great sense of compassion for her that I had never felt before.

It helped to explain all the stonewalling and I'm afraid, many of her lies or projections, as well. Lies designed to protect herself from experiencing such "blunt force trauma" again (I say that metaphorically and not in any other way).

She just does not want to go back and experience where she was and the things that happened to her. She found a way to cope by burying them and moving on. It seemed to work, until this Twin Flame connection, this dynamic, came up with me, and like all true Twin Flame connections, everything is exposed, and all the dark shadows start coming to light throughout the process, and they keep coming up over and over again to the surface. As we have learned, they must be effectively dealt with when they come up, or they'll keep coming up over and over again.

So, when your perception, outlook, or attitude is..."Why does he (or she) get off easy and I have to do *all* the work?" I want you to please keep in mind that you cannot see the work he or she is doing. I also want you to keep in mind, you don't know what earthly burdens your Twin has carried in this lifetime that you don't even know about. We Divine Feminines (DFs) have a "hard row to hoe," too (don't get me wrong), but our burdens (and our roles) are very different from theirs. We are handling (for now) more of the 5-D connection and the purging, healing, and conversations with God, the angels, and our guides. Us

DFs have learned to find comfort and solace there and we now know how to more effectively navigate the ins and outs of this Journey.

Meanwhile, in many cases, the DM is still "in the fog" somewhat and trying to see his or her way out. Much is becoming clearer, but they are just now getting the opportunity to see some of the things we saw and experienced earlier in our Journeys.

This may be why, if you are at this point, you may be hearing more songs and getting more "synchs" from the earlier part of your Journey, when you were first learning about Twins and the connection, what it meant, and you also had the great feelings of love, but you were in a tailspin trying to take all the disparate pieces of the puzzle and put them into something that made sense. Remember that stage?

So, when you get into this mode of judging and comparing, just try to stop. The truth is that attitude or positioning is just reflecting more of the martyrdom/victim energy mentality, and that is something for you to continue looking at and shedding.

If that's coming up for you, I suggest you meditate, reflect, acknowledge, purge and heal those aspects of your Self.

Remember, as I say, in the first *Twin Flame Guidebook: Your Practical Guide to Navigating the Journey (Book One)*, this is a co-creative process. Between you and your Twin Flame. Designed and signed off on, by you and your Twin, before you ever incarnated here in the Earthly realm. Your Twin is doing his/her part and you are doing yours. Everything is as it should be.

Your Twin is also "playing [his or her] role" perfectly. The Journey was designed to elicit in both of you a reaction or response to trigger your core wounding and to help you awaken, heal, and ascend. That's what this is all about.

Moving Forward

Are You Feeling Restless?

One of the early, telltale signs of the Twin Flame Journey (and it may occur later, as well, is a feeling of restlessness). I mentioned it to my Twin early on, that I was having feelings of restlessness, but I didn't know why. She later echoed that same sentiment back to me a few months later. (Like a mirror.) But I think she wasn't conscious of that fact, that the feeling had bounced off of me and over to her. (Or perhaps vice versa.)

This restless feeling comes about because you are no longer resonating in your existing 3-D life. You are asking for a change. You are asking for more light, more positivity, more happiness, and more joy. You are expanding, just like the expansive power and nature of the Universe.

You recognize and realize you cannot get that or achieve those states in your present reality, in your current circumstances. And that is because you constructed your present reality when you were in a lower vibrational state, before you awakened. Where things were more restricted.

The only way to get beyond the restlessness is to identify what you want and how you want your life to be, feel, and look. Who and what do you want to be? Who do you see yourself with, as you discover and embody your true, authentic Self?

Vision Board

I found it helpful at this stage to construct a vision board. I cut out various images from magazines that resonated with me across a variety of topics and themes (nature, finances, career/vocation, love, etc.) and I purchased a foam core board at a local arts and crafts supply store.

Working as fast as I could, without letting my analytical mind get involved, I placed and pasted the images where I thought they "felt" the best. When I was done, I was ecstatic about this beautiful piece of very customized artwork that represented my current hopes, dreams, and aspirations. It was MY vision board. And it's served as a touchstone to guide my life. When I feel down or confused or lost on my Journey, I look at that board. I create one board each year. It's rewarding to see how my life has since transformed for the better since making my vision boards. I guess you could say it is the visual equivalent of putting affirming Post-it notes on your bathroom mirror that you repeat to yourself every day.

Try it and see how your life transforms in new and exciting ways.

A Trip to Joyland

Remember that feeling you had early on the Twin Flame Journey when you couldn't get enough of your Twin, when you were having the time of your life, when you were experiencing the most fun you had ever had, and felt the best you have ever felt with another person? When the two of you were stuck together like glue, very magnetic and attractive (or attracting) to one another, like a magnet.

Well, guess what? It's time to rediscover that sense of fun and joy—whether with or without your Twin—whether you are together, or in Separation.

This is critical to keeping your vibration high, and your Twin can feel whether you are in a high-vibrational state, or a lower vibrational state. He or she can feel it, and he or she may need that lift that only you can provide, when you find and rediscover joy for yourself.

How can you do this when you are feeling the pain of Separation, or the virtually bottomless lows of the "Dark Night of the Soul," or "DNOTS?"

There are many ways you can do this and here are just a few suggestions:

1. Think of your Beloved and all the great times and memories that you have shared together.

2. Hang out with a friend or friends you enjoy. Pick those people who "feel like sunshine." If the person typically brings you down, choose a different friend. The ones who make you feel light, airy, and happy are best for rediscovering joy.

3. Make time for yourself. Set aside time each week that is just FOR YOU, that is wholly dedicated to whatever YOU want to do.

4. Get away for a day-trip or a weekend (or even a long weekend). If budget is an issue, you can find free or low-cost events in your community. Pick up your community paper or newsweekly and see what events there are. (Note: This book was written partially prior to COVID-19, so please keep that in mind.)

5. Laugh more. Put on a comedy you haven't seen. Go to a comedy show in your town.

6. Go see live music. Music is the universal language. Listening to great music, dancing, and supporting local performers and artists is good for the soul.

7. Get out into nature. There's nothing more soul-soothing than a good walk in the woods, or near the water, or in a place that brings you peace. Take a friend, or go it alone. Sometimes the alone time is just what the doctor ordered!

8. Volunteer for a non-profit or for something to benefit people or your community. Nothing brings the heart joy like being in service to others.

Staying happy, healthy, and light only makes you more attractive to your Twin (and if your Twin isn't currently "an option"), it will make you more attractive to others, as well.

Fixed Things Versus Fluid Things

In the 3-D, we've gotten very used to things being firm, concrete, hard, and inflexible. If someone is "done with you," "forever," in the old 3-D mindset/construct, that would mean, "I'm done with you now, forever and always…don't bother me in this life again." It would be a sign-off, the kiss of death, the most permanent state of affairs and being that one could imagine.

A recent message I've received from my guides is that things are far more flexible and fluid than we previously thought. Things can change on a dime: Emotions, feelings, situations, and hard and established positions.

That is because the higher dimensions are being anchored down into the 3-D dimension. Though we're still living in the 3-D reality with all the constants and givens we've grown used to…gravity, etc., we're moving from a more "matter-based" realm to one that is more thought-based, more energy-based. You know yourself that your thoughts are fleeting. What you feel one day, one minute or one second may change 100% to the next day. Our experience in this realm will become more like that.

Sadly, this shift is threatening to many people and to the former hierarchies and modes of being. The entire 3-D world operates on fact, on concrete reality. And once a position was set, or an impression of someone given, it "stuck." Not anymore. People aren't believing everything they see, hear, feel, taste, and touch. The old illusions are falling away. People are feeling into things more with their hearts. Even though they still listen with their heads and logic still has a place, it's not as prominent as the heart-based experience of the world that is coming forth right now in our time.

What does this feel like in our 3-D experience? Belief in miracles, gratitude for every experience (even the "bad ones"), seeing things in the most positive light. Believing that people and circumstances *can* change for the better. Feeling confident. Feeling hopeful. Feeling creative. Feeling LOVE. Believing in possibilities. Having hope. Giving people and yourself the benefit of the doubt. Seeing the most in people and situations.

We have the power to change in the moment. We have the power to co-create in the moment. Every moment is both choice and opportunity. This experience in life, on Earth, can be virtually ANYTHING we wish it to be.

How do we think humans discovered the ability to fly? How we discovered and succeeded in going into outer space and even moving toward other planets? The dream- and vision-space that we allowed ourselves to be in gave birth to those dreams...which became manifestations in reality. But someone had to FEEL it first. Perhaps someone

DREAMED it first. After all, dreams do have an energetic signature that we still feel upon waking and dreams have fueled probably every advancement known to humankind.

So, if things look bleak in your life, or in your own personal Journey, take heart. It will be okay. And anything, and EVERYTHING is possible.

Past Lives (Alternate Lifetimes)

Reincarnation, the ability to come back into this world after death and be born again at some point with the same soul, incarnated in a different body, is a belief that many people and many religions hold. Reincarnation is a primary tenet of Indian religions, including Buddhism, Sikhism, and Hinduism. Many streams of Orthodox Judaism also believe in it, as well as the native North Americans. Some indigenous Australians also believe in it, while historic Greek figures such as Pythagoras, Socrates, and Plato also subscribed to the concept. In recent decades, the belief in reincarnation has gained a greater foothold in Europe and North America.

In my experience, it's critical to be aware of past lives/ alternate lifetimes if you are on the Twin Flame Journey. For some of you, you will have shared hundreds, if not thousands, of past life experiences with your Twin.

At some point on my Journey, I was working on one of our rental properties and Alexa, the home speaker from Amazon, randomly came on (though I didn't have it turned "on") and started playing a popular song from 1910 who many people (including Bing Crosby in 1934 and 1944) have covered and performed over time (I later learned), but I had never consciously heard this song. It was a song called, "Let Me Call You Sweetheart" and it came, like some song-gem from a mysterious and unknown prior time and lifetime, into that particular moment.

I listened to the lyrics and then looked them up and this particular song had a very powerful message for me. I later confirmed with my pendulum that this particular song has some significance to a past life, and the pendulum also confirmed that it was a past life with my Twin. I had intuitively felt the song, its message, and its lyrics was a message from her, intended for me. Some people would call this crazy, and I know that (and I consciously recognize it), but the song came out of the blue, inexplicably. You see, no one in my family (where we have the account with Alexa) would ever play a song from that era. It wasn't in the search history or algorithm. If you're a true Twin on the path, you know things like this sometimes happen, inexplicable things, and there is a reason for them.

It's better to accept, smile, and move on, but I do believe these things happen to remind you of the love you once shared, and also as an affirmation to keep going, stay on the path, and in the immortal words of Journey (my favorite band, always): "Don't stop believin'".

But, for those of you who care to read the lyrics, here they are:

"Let Me Call You Sweetheart"

I am dreaming, Dear, of you, day by day
Dreaming when the skies are blue, when they're gray
When the silv'ry moonlight gleams,
Still I wander on in dreams
In a land of love, it seems
Just with you

Chorus:
Let me call you, "Sweetheart," I'm in love with you
Let me hear you whisper that you love me, too
Keep the love-light glowing in your eyes so true
Let me call you, "Sweetheart," I'm in love with you

Longing for you, all the while, more and more
Longing for the sunny smile, I adore
Birds are singing far and near, roses blooming ev'rywhere
You, alone, my heart can cheer; You, just you...

But back to reincarnation and past lives, sometimes what is going on with you and your Twin will not be easy to explain on the surface, or just by looking at the regular, 3-D experience. Indeed, there is much you sometimes cannot explain, such as why one person behaves in a certain way, and why you react in a certain way. And that is where figuring out past lives, what role you played, what each of you did to the other, the dynamics...what transpired...can be valuable. Clearing out old energetic blockages, karmic patterns, and karma itself can be very beneficial to helping you evolve and progress on your Journey and in your Twin Flame dynamic.

One of my very good friends does past life readings for Twins, as well as the general public. Her work has helped many people uncover and unlock the secrets and mysteries of their lives in many ways, and it has also helped many Twin Flames locate the puzzle pieces that they need to place within their ever-evolving jigsaw puzzle.

Just a few examples: You and your Divine Counterpart may have had a past life in the Roman or Greek era in which one of you sold one of your children that you had together as a slave in exchange for money (because of political reasons). Obviously, there would be vast karma lingering as a result of that. Or one of you during the Victorian Era of England may have institutionalized the other, for whatever reason. Again, that's some heavy karma to surface and transmute. Yet another past life may have been a Native American couple having a miscarriage in the American Plains during the 1800s. And in yet another life, you and your Twin may have been relatives of the other (in order to learn certain lessons) and those dynamics, patterns, and blueprints may carry over into this lifetime. The possibilities are endless, and the karma is real. What you do to each other in one lifetime can carry over to the next, and also those imprinted experiences can remain in your energy field(s) to be cleared out at a later date. If you are not conscious of these experiences and relationships and connections, they remain; however, if you learn of them...by making the unconscious conscious, that can go a long way in clearing out blockages, negative patterns, imprints, and karma.

Like the friend I mentioned, there are professionals who focus on Past Life Readings/Regressions and/or Akashic

Records readings. These people can help you figure out who you and your Twin might have been in a past relationship dynamic. This may help you shed light on why things are unfolding today in the way that they are. Sometimes, glimpses of past lives can even come through to you during your own meditations, by yourself. Don't be surprised if this happens. Just accept what comes through. In fact, you can open yourself up to receiving more of this information by setting simple intentions around receiving or perceiving past life experiences. And if you need help from someone else, by all means, seek it. The answers you will receive will be invaluable as you continue on your Journey, and as you seek to figure out the "why" of it all, why he or she is avoiding you, why he or she is running from you, why he or she is chasing you, and why your interactions go in the way they do.

Just like in life, when we understand the history of it all, we can figure out the mystery of it all and we can be so much more successful in navigating all of it. I didn't understand any of this as it related to my Journey until recently, and I have such a better understanding of it now, which has helped me not only to heal, but to relax and release and to allow the Journey to unfold in the way in which it will. To keep it simple, my learning about our past lives has helped me surrender to the divine Journey and to "let go and let God." From another song, from another era: "Que sera, sera": "Whatever will be, will be."

Ode to Karmics

A key part of virtually every Twin Flame Journey is the karmic, or a karmic, or karmics. I say it that way because it can be more than one thing serving as an obstacle to you and your Beloved reuniting in this lifetime. It can be another person, or a demanding or toxic job, or even an addiction to something, such as alcohol and/or drugs. It can be the relationship your Twin has with his or her mother, or his or her father, or another family member. The bottom line: "The karmic" serves to delay or prevent the two of you from coming together.

The Beloved will usually be very beholden to this thing, no matter how it presents itself. And that will be for a variety of reasons. It can be a marriage or partnership, of course, and as we all know, there is a lot of societal programming around marriages and partnerships, and for some good reasons, though at times, there are times when the relationship is no longer serving the person and it's best for it to be let go of, in appropriate ways.

The karmic can be a demanding or toxic job, but your Beloved keeps it because he or she has worked hard to attain a certain level of status, or he or she may have obligations that require them to remain in the proverbial "hamster wheel." The karmic can be addiction to drugs and/or alcohol, and your Beloved may be physically or emotionally addicted to substances that help them escape reality in certain ways. Family relationships can also present obstacles, particularly if there are age or cultural or religious differences between the counterparts. Family and cultural (and even religious) programming can be very strong and difficult to break free from. But when it is no longer in a person's best interest, he or she may begin moving in a different direction and close out that karmic cycle (or those karmic cycles).

Oftentimes, when our Beloved has a karmic, in the initial stages of our Journey, we may dislike this person or situation or circumstance. We may "rail" against it. We may feel it is an enemy to us as it stands in the way of what we most want (and what we feel we deserve).

The truth is, your Twin's karmic is your karmic, too, in the sense the person or situation is a life lesson for your Twin to learn and grow from. When your Twin is learning and growing from his or her karmic (or when your Twin is being harmed by the karmic), that presents lessons and opportunity. And with those lessons and opportunity come Soul Growth for your Twin. That is how you and your Twin learn, grow, and change. That is how we evolve.

So, instead of hating on the karmic, or trying to remove the karmic from both of your lives, just let your Twin have the experience that he or she has chosen (to the extent that is reasonable, unless it is a life-threatening situation or circumstance). There are soul lessons your Twin can only get from these other avenues, and for their Journeys to be complete, they must finish the soul lessons for which they signed up. When you look at karmics with this perspective, perhaps it will make it easier to bear and endure.

"Love it the Way it is"

So, you may not like where you are in your Journey right now. But you've traveled through hundreds, if not thousands, of lifetimes to get to this exact teaching moment. This exact moment. Maybe it's an email or a voice mail or something you hear from a mutual friend that rips you to shreds. Or you learn of another's betrayal. See the instance, the person, the thing, as the lesson. Notice it. And appreciate it for what it is.

You have manifested your Twin and these instances to teach you these difficult lessons.

I remember once in yoga class, at the end, where they have you do a brief meditation. During my post-workout meditation, a single word about my Twin came into the landscape of my mind, and it was the word, "Teacher." I don't know why it came to me just then, but it did, and it was immediately clear to me that it was a message relative to my Twin. (Remember: The teacher always shows up when the student is ready.) When I walked outside right after class, I received an email from my Divine Counterpart. "I'm not comfortable," she said.

And it, and what she shared, was devastating, but I had the word "teacher" burned into my brain from the meditation. And yes, she was and is my teacher (at least, one of them). And yes, the lesson was (and remains) harsh. But it was the lesson for me: The lesson to learn to accept it all and love myself nonetheless. The lesson of not internalizing what my Twin was (or is) saying to me. Throughout the Journey and all its broad, deep, and rich lessons, you'll come to realize that because of God's love, you are whole, and nothing—no one, nor anyone's words, or opinions—can harm you. This direct message I've just stated came to me after another particularly difficult exchange with my counterpart and now, I impart it to you.

Try saying that to yourself a few times: "Because of God's love, I am whole, and nothing can harm me. Not my Twin. Not anyone."

That is a liberating affirmation.

Back to your current situation, whatever it may be, keep this in mind:

"Love it the way it is."

This is a line from a book by Ram Dass on spiritual awakening and meditation. It's the perfect statement for this moment, and for every moment that unfolds with your counterpart.

Reconnecting to Your Self

The world is awash with people who are disconnected from Self and you are seeing this play out on the world stage right now, in virtually every area of life.

It was Plato who said, "Know thyself." It seems like such a simple statement, and yet it is very profound in its implications.

Do I *really* know myself? Do you *really* know yourself?

I was asked the question recently by Lee Patterson (Lee and Sherry Patterson of "Relationship Reinvented"): How are you disconnected from Self?

Strangely enough, I didn't have an answer. Why is that? How could I be so disconnected that I couldn't even answer such a simple question? But it's true. I stammered. I paused. I pretty I much told Lee I'd have to get back to him on that.

And it wasn't immediately obvious. Until it was.

What I came to realize is that I was so disconnected from Self that I couldn't have told you that I was unhappy in my relationship over the last 20 years. I couldn't quite put my finger on it. Just that something felt "off." When I looked back to certain events or things that should have made me happy (like travel or a trip), I couldn't feel joy in those moments. Why couldn't I feel joy in those moments? Because I wasn't happy. I wasn't happy with the relationship. I wasn't happy with how I felt with my karmic partner. But most important, I wasn't happy with my SELF. I now realize after much self-reflection that I couldn't have been happy with this person or even with my own Self because I wasn't in ALIGNMENT with my truest, highest Self. Through many years of self-reflection and meditation, I've finally been able to become more in ALIGNMENT with my Self and my purpose and mission on Earth. (It's an evolving process, by the way.) This means I've been able to strengthen the connection to my Self.

This also means I was able to now articulate my feelings back then and attach words to them. The word "unhappy" most comes to mind. It's so interesting. Many of us are so disconnected from Self we don't know how we feel most of the time. We don't acknowledge how we feel. We don't know how to put words to a feeling.

This is a step to self-mastery, being able to recognize our feelings, put words to them, and share and release them. Otherwise, these emotions hold more power for us and stick around much longer than they probably should.

Something that is meant to wash in and wash out like a wave or a current...stays. It remains, and then it "gunks" up your emotional body, throwing the whole thing out of alignment. (You can, of course, clear it up with meditations or a certified Reiki healer or other healing modalities, by the way.)

Every day, try to work to strengthen your connection to your Self. Sometimes the hardest thing to do is to pick ourselves. Our Twin cannot pick us unless they first choose themselves. This means letting go of pleasing others, letting go of karmic situations, letting go of "shadow emotions" like judgment and shame, letting go of being worried about what others will think of us. Perhaps it also means stepping out of the spiritual closet.

Focus on yourself. Acknowledge, articulate, and share your emotions. In this way, you can become a brighter, lighter better version of your Self. You can truly come to know yourself, which will positively impact every relationship you have for the rest of your life.

Alignment & Ascension

So, I think many of us think our Twin or our Beloved, is the end-all, be-all. And he or she may be. But what this Journey has taught me (and brought me) is that the Journey is also (if not equally, or more) about our getting into alignment with the Divine Mind and Divine Will and also the Ascension process. If you haven't been following Ascension and higher dimensional topics on YouTube, then you may want to start, because if you are a true Twin Flame, that is the path that you are on.

You see, the Journey helps burn away all of us that is not 100 percent true and authentic. All the falsehoods, all the masks, all the drama, all the ego. As you undergo the Journey, you cannot carry these old 3-D falsehoods, personas, and experiences along with you. Out the window goes victimhood. Out the window goes addiction and co-dependencies. In comes your authentic, true Self. In comes your independence and sovereignty. In comes your spiritual Soul Growth and transformation. And there's no going back. (You wouldn't want to, anyway, once you see the beauty of things as they really are, and once you see the real truth of things, of all things.) The Ascension process helps you see things that you couldn't see previously. It helps you to see things more as the

Divine does, free of judgment, free of hatred, free of anger, free of vengeance. It helps you come to terms and peace with "a time for all seasons."

To everything, there is a season,
A time for every purpose under heaven:

A time to be born and a time to die;
A time to plant and a time to pluck what is planted;
A time to kill and a time to heal;
A time to break down and a time to build up;
A time to weep and a time to laugh;
A time to mourn and a time to dance;
A time to cast away stones and a time to gather stones;
A time to embrace and a time to refrain from embracing;
A time to gain and a time to lose;
A time to keep and a time to throw away;
A time to tear and a time to sew;
A time to keep silence and a time to speak;
A time to love and a time to hate;
A time of war and a time of peace.

The Bible: Ecclesiastes 3: 2-8

Intention

As my Reiki Master has taught me, everything begins and ends with intention. Before you undertake any project or any assignment, any job, any task, or any role or function in life, before you go on a date, before you have an important meeting or conversation, before you take off on a trip, be sure to set your intentions for whatever it is you are about to do.

I also find if you write it down, it can be particularly powerful. Setting your intentions down on paper is an important way to start your day, your week, your month, or your year. (Writing it down is also a powerful way to manifest what it is that you seek and want to attract into your life.)

For example, say if you have a planned trip to London, your list of intentions might look like this. I'll use a recent example specific to me, but please adjust to your own projects/work. If you'd like, you can also use "SMART" goals (Specific, Measurable, Attainable, Relevant, and Timely).

1) Place my book in one or two independent book-shops by the time I depart London.
2) Talk with three people about my book.
3) Hold one book signing event.

4) Meet like-minded people who are passionate about my subject area(s).
5) Go sight-seeing to two important tourist destinations.

You can also meditate or ruminate on your intentions or your planned meeting or trip to go more deeply into your subconscious and unearth your wants and needs. As part of this process, you can also use visualization to envision yourself having the successful meeting, project, or trip. Many athletes (such as basketball's Michael Jordan) have used visualization techniques to be more successful in their sport (making the three-point shot, making the foul shot).

If you believe it, you truly can achieve it. And belief is the prerequisite for actually doing. If a person does not believe, then there is no way an individual can achieve something or do something, whether it's obtaining your Twin, or achieving a life goal, completing a bucket-list item, or getting the job you've always dreamed of, or taking the trip of a lifetime. It's true that "thoughts are things." First you must think it to manifest it. Something cannot be manifested unless at first it exists in the form of thought.

First, your wish or your desire comes into conscious view. Once it becomes conscious, you use thought to shape it, to fill in the space with colors and vivid details. Once you get to this level of imagining and truly believe that something can come to fruition (and you can imagine it and experience it as if it is so), then you are very powerful indeed. A powerful manifestor. A powerful creator.

Integration

I took some time to ruminate on this topic: integration. It's a very important one. When you are on the Journey, and then you later go into a Separation period, and you cannot feel your Divine Counterpart as closely, this is because your Twin has become more closely aligned to you, and within you.

Once you have integrated more of your Twin's energy, whether a Divine Masculine or a Divine Feminine, you will not feel him or her quite as much, because the two of you are now more in alignment with the other one. This explains why you don't "feel" him or her as much. You don't feel the difference in the energetic field as much. There is no longer dissonance between your energetic signatures. Inner union and the balance between the two of you is coming more into play, and more into reality. And once the scales balance, it can mean smoother sailing. Whether or not you're in Separation, you'll still have the ability to share mental telepathy with one another and you can still communicate in the 5-D/astral plane.

One time, after I had been on my Journey for a couple of years, I was eating out with friends at an upscale restaurant in a neighboring town, and I could very strongly feel the energy of my Twin coming in, and it was as if she was actually there, physically, in the restaurant. The restaurant had three different floors, so I excused myself and went to the restroom, and casually went around the three floors to see if she was there. I could feel her so strongly, it was overpowering.

Because I didn't see her in the physical (the truth is, I didn't really expect to, but the energy was so intense and overpowering), I used my pendulum—which is connected to my guides and therefore, I use for divination assistance—later that night to ask whether my Twin was indeed in the restaurant. My pendulum indicated she was. I was puzzled by that answer. Knowing I had really looked for her and she wasn't there in the 3-D, I laughed and asked my pendulum if it was now counting us as the same person. It answered in the affirmative with a speedy "Yes," and I had to chuckle again.

Our energy signature has come into an internal union of sorts and therefore, it is no longer separate. That is why I can no longer feel her as clearly, though at times, when I am in more of a doubting phase, then it makes it easier to chalk all this up to an overactive imagination and a very bad case of unrequited love. Again, as I said in *The Twin Flame Guidebook* (Book One), it's very easy to get in this mode of doubt and disbelief because of instances such as this. But this Journey is nothing if not a Journey of faith and patient endurance. Those are the keys to mastering this Journey. Mastery of the Mind, Mastery of the Self, Mastery of Your Own Energy and understanding it for what it is, and what it is becoming.

Time to Make a Different Choice

If You're Not Going to Do Personal Work...

When you're on a Twin Flame Journey, work toward your own personal self-development and Soul Growth is a mandatory requirement for the Journey to work and for it to progress and move forward. I am in contact with quite a few Twins and those who do the work are usually able to come into Union with both polarities of themselves, both the masculine polarity and the feminine polarity. Once you are more balanced inside your own Self, then it's possible that your Twin will follow suit and move into greater alignment as well. It is only through both partners doing the work that Union is possible.

I do know of Twins who do not wish to do the work, or who, for whatever reason, do not "do" the work. Who do not wish to change, even when something is brought to their attention and floated up through their subconscious mind to their conscious mind. From these people, you would typically hear all types of excuses such as "I'm not going to change;" or "I don't see how this would ever work;" or even, and I hear this a lot in my work with Twins: "I don't even *like* certain aspects of my Twin." All very normal.

We must always remember that our Twins are mirroring "our stuff" right back to us. They are designed to perfectly trigger us in the ways that will help us with our development and growth (and vice versa). There is a particular responsibility of Divine Feminines to lead the way in seeing the patterns, recognizing the soul lessons, and then working to clear those blockages and to balance aspects of the connection. That is our job. For the Divine Masculine, their job is to again, trigger us perfectly and help us grow, but also to ground many aspects of the relationship into the 3-D. To be clear, both Twins share the duty of grounding the connection firmly into the 3-D. Each Twin has a role to play.

If you choose not to do anything or to change in any way, of course, that is your right and your ability to do so. Through free will, you'll always be able to choose.

But don't expect the connection to "magically" work itself out if neither of you is doing the work. You can only control what you can control, though, and that is your portion of the connection. Your connection to Self, and your connection to your Twin.

When you don't do the work, you are short-circuiting the connection and in essence, "shorting it out." It's like an electrical current. If it's not grounded, the electricity doesn't flow, and it will short-circuit. The connection cannot work if no one is doing the work. Likewise, the connection cannot work also if it is one-sided, with only one Twin doing the work.

There are many possible outcomes to your Twin Flame connection:

1) You realize the Twin Flame connection to your Divine Counterpart, but you sit back and "do nothing." You don't do the work. Perhaps you don't even reach out to the other. The connection sits, stagnant. Nothing progresses and it becomes an interesting fact of your life that you don't really share with anyone other than yourself. Perhaps your Soul Plan is not realized as you cannot connect to your Twin, nor to your Divine guidance or shared Life Purpose and Soul Mission.

2) You realize the Twin Flame connection, you take the steps necessary to work on your blocks, insecurities, wounds, and inner child issues. You grow and develop greatly, in all aspects of your life. You are more balanced and whole. You become more connected to Self. You and your Twin may or may not come into Divine Union together (depending on whether your Twin is "plugged in" and connected and doing the work also), but your life is more fulfilled because of all the work you did, on your own. Perhaps you pursue your Soul Mission on your own. Your impact on the world is significant. When you look back on your life, you feel proud and like you "left the world a little better than you found it."

3) Both you and your Twin realize and acknowledge the connection. You both take the steps necessary to overcome what is blocking the connection and achieve a beautiful, balanced, blissful energy together,

enabling you to come together in Divine Union. You grow together in all aspects of your combined life. You both become balanced and whole. You become more connected to Self and one another. You create, in essence, "Heaven on Earth" through your relationship, through your connection. You both are able to accomplish your Life Purpose and Soul Mission, together. Your impact on the world is far greater than had you did it all alone. When you look back on your life and your connection, you feel proud and like the two of you did all you could to make a positive, significant impact on the world. The story is whole, complete.

As Twin Flames, we are privileged to experience this Sacred Love and beyond-special connection. But with this privilege does come great responsibility and duty. Remember, you and/or your soul chose this path before you even incarnated. You chose it to become the highest and best version of yourself. You chose it to fully feel the love of your Divine Partner, your beautiful Twin. You chose this path to not only feel the beautiful and unconditional love of your Divine Counterpart, but you ultimately did it to grow closer to God in all His/Her glory. It's the path back to yourself. The path to your Beloved. The path back to God. It's an awesome responsibility, but YOU entrusted yourself with it. You are big enough. You are amazing enough. You can do it. No regrets.

"It's the Way it Had to Be"

Last night, I did something new for the first time. I purged like crazy while I was sleeping. I was dreaming that my Twin and I were in the same environment, around a lot of different people, like at a party, where there were many different pockets of people and areas where we could go. Well, much like the latest turn of events in the 3-D, she was avoiding me at every turn. I had hoped we would get to talk, but she evaded me. This sent me into a crying jag, like guttural crying in my dream, so palpable I could feel it emerging into my physical body and consciousness. It went on and on and on, and it was very intense and emotional.

I consciously said to myself in my dream-state, "Wow, I'm really purging...and in a dream, too." In the 3-D, I am not much for crying, but I was really letting loose in this dream.

Then, as I was between wake and sleep, I thought about how cruel my Twin had/has been to me in many instances. I thought about how cruel the Twins of others close to me have also been. I thought about the trauma inflicted by the Journey. And the message came through that this was actually very necessary and "it was the way it had to be."

You see, in the 3-D, our Twins may have been cruel to us, they may have been extreme to us, and their responses to us often didn't match up to what was happening. Meaning their reactions were sometimes much more intense than was called for "in the real world." (At least, that was my experience and the experience of many close friends I have talked to about the Journey.) The guidance coming through to me last night was that it had to be so, in order that the polarities could be worked out. Say, as one example, you wrote an innocent and pure email with good intent to your Twin encouraging them not to date someone else or to get engaged to another person. (Just as a hypothetical example.) And your Twin then "blasted" you with a lengthy email that basically destroyed you in every way, calling out every negative thought you've ever had about yourself, every insecurity. And you know his or her response in no way matched up to the note you sent. You triggered something very deep and real inside him or her. Then they sought to break you down with words or actions. In my case, my Twin sought to decimate me and break me down to the point I could no longer stand up, so to speak.

But, guess what? I rose. I rose and met her again with unconditional love and her request for me not to contact her was, of course, honored (until COVID-19 set in). That outreach didn't work out, on the surface. But I still sent (and send) unconditional love her way. And I still do.

It had to be this way. She and our Twins had to meet us with such fierce force as to engage the polarity that we, as Divine Feminines, needed to neutralize. We're not just purging and transmuting for ourselves or for the Collectives: We're purging and transmuting for the entirety of humanity.

The entire human history. Every bad thing that has ever happened, that has ever been experienced, or been said. All the pain. All the loss. All the disappointment. We are neutralizing it all throughout our Journey, bringing it to the zero point, and zeroing it out.

"It had to be so" because this is how the Journey is designed. It's not designed to elicit romantic love, though that happens in many cases. While helping all of humanity sounds lofty and some might consider it "delusional," it's designed to provide a service to humanity that would otherwise not be provided. Through the Twins and their commitment to serve as Lightworkers. Through the Twins and their soul agreements before we incarnated.

Had the interactions, or the Journey, been simple, and smooth sailing all the way through, it would have just been "another love story." Another happy ending. But that's not necessarily all we sought to do when we planned to incarnate again here on Earth, in the 3-D.

That's why it's so damn hard. That's why it's so soul-crushing at times. It is our mission as Divine Feminines to transmute all of this negative emotion, this negative energy, to meet it with our positive, loving charges fueled by unconditional love. And to help our Twin feel that love, no matter what. And to rise again even though it seems impossible. And to rise again, even when we thought we couldn't. And to rise again, even though we've been decimated in every way. All our ego, all our drama, all our hang-ups melted away, burned away, leaving only the essence of unconditional love. That is our Divine Purpose, that is our Divine Mission and together, we rise.

Heartbroken

One of the energies you'll no doubt be dealing with throughout your Journey—and indeed, if you're reading this, you may be feeling this right now—is the energy of heartbreak, or being heartbroken. This is not an easy or fun energy to manage.

You may be heartbroken about the way things turned out with your Twin. You may be heartbroken about experiencing the loss of them, whether it's been a real loss, such as them passing away, or the temporary—and illusionary—loss of Separation from your Twin in the 3-D.

We cannot be disconnected from our Twin. We are always connected through our Energy Body and in the Higher Realms. Feelings of disconnection and Separation are an illusion, though they feel very persistent and real at times.

Perhaps you're in a "no contact" situation with your Twin, whether you initiated it, or he or she did. Recognize that that is okay, and it is part of your Journey. It is not permanent, and you can never be truly disconnected or separated from your Twin. The energetic exchanges and communications continue to happen whether you are in 3-D communication, or not.

So, if they ask you not to contact them, you can respond in the affirmative *("Sure, no problem. No worries. I won't be contacting you again")* knowing that your connection as Twins is secure…always, and that it is continuing to happen in various ways, and cannot be broken. Now, this fact angers some, particularly Twin "runners" who do not wish to be tethered or tied to another in this way. If this describes you, then please look at those emotions, evaluate them, and ask yourself, "Why?" "Why am I running from this connection?" and "What am I actually running away from?" In this way, you'll hopefully be able to get to the root of the issue and to heal it, process it, and move forward (or move on) in a way that is meaningful and productive for you. These emotions are meant to happen. They are meant to be felt, to give us clues and insight into our Inner Being and to bring us into alignment with the Divine and our Highest Selves. When you can experience an emotion and no longer look at it as a "bad thing," when you can look at it in a neutral way and understand what that emotion or that feeling is trying to show you, then you can unlock many mysteries about yourself (that were previously unexplained), and you'll be one step closer to happiness, healthiness, and wholeness, not to mention peace.

None of the Journey is "bad." None of the emotions you'll experience (even heartbrokenness) are "bad," though they can make you feel very uncomfortable. The point of the Journey, the lessons, are all about learning. Learning new ways to be. Learning new ways to explore and express yourself. Reaching a higher level than you thought you could previously attain. Loving your Self. And loving others. Healing the wounds that haunt you, whether they're your wounds, wounds you've inherited from your family or others, or ancestral wounds that cling to us over time.

At some point of your Journey, you will feel heartbroken. You will feel as if you can never truly LIVE or LOVE again. But that is also illusion. You are always loved. You are never separated from Source. You are never separated from your Divine Counterpart. In all ways, you are always connected to the infinite and unconditional LOVE of Spirit, of Source Energy. Let that knowledge and that awareness enter your heart and fill you up. Sit with it. Really feel it. Meditate and go into that space of heart awareness. Go to nature. Be with it. Allow your heart (and your Self) to expand. Feel the freeing energy of THAT. The freeing energy of that which is timeless, which is limitless, which is infinite and loving beyond understanding.

Miracles

I put a post on Facebook talking about the power of miracles. I have probably at least 1,600 or more Facebook contacts; to be frank, I'm not actually sure. I actually grabbed the meme from something else I saw and liked and personalized it with my own message about how many times I have been saved by a miracle, and noted all the times I was probably also saved and didn't even know about it.

I want you to know, that aside from my own Mother, only a handful of other people felt comfortable (or took the time) to write their own personal miracles out. Maybe they did, indeed, experience miracles, but they didn't feel comfortable sharing on the very public platform of Facebook.

That said something to me: that we are very uncomfortable in this 3-D realm talking about things of a spiritual nature. There is so much societal and religious programming, as well as good ol' fashioning bullying or mockery, that makes people feel compelled to keep these sorts of things very close to their chest. Or worse yet, maybe they don't believe in miracles at all.

But that makes me very sad on a whole lot of different levels. Are we so disconnected from the Divine that we cannot even recognize a miracle when we see one? Are we so afraid of others' reactions that we won't even talk about it or acknowledge it?

What are we so afraid of?

Obviously, the silence has brought up so many questions for me, more questions than answers. But, it's troubling to me. That we are so disconnected from Source, so disconnected from all the miraculous events in our lives, or at the very least, unable or unwilling to talk about them.

I do believe that Twin Flames are here to make the world a bit better, however and wherever we can. And that it is our duty to share these messages. That people are not alone. That they are divinely protected oftentimes, many times, most of the time. I believe that our free will may, in fact, be given precedence at times over Divine Intervention and Divine Will, but I also know Divine Intervention is real. And I know it comes when I ask for it. And I acknowledge the truth of "Ask and ye shall receive."

Two Critical Soul Lessons

There are two indisputable Soul Lessons (and one could say, requirements) of the Twin Flame Journey and moving into a higher dimensional way of being and living. Those two Soul Lessons are: 1) Self-Love, and 2) Sovereignty. No Twin Flame path, Journey, or Union is complete without both partners realizing and achieving these two states of being.

Self-Love

Self-Love is the acknowledgement and acceptance of yourself as a Divine Being. It is the stripping away of all the ways in which you beat yourself down or let others beat you down. It requires you to stand up for yourself. After all, if you aren't going to stand up for yourself, who will? Self-Love requires you to love yourself as much as you have ever loved another. It is not a state you can get to if you are still in co-dependent patterns. It is not a state you can get to if you are abusing yourself in any way, or allowing others to abuse you. It is not a state you can get to if you are following addictive pursuits or self-sabotaging pursuits. It is your natural state of being and the ultimate state of being, in a way, because it is the beginning and end of all relationships you will have, meaning, you cannot truly have a fulfilling, healthy, and whole relationship with *anyone* if you do not love yourself, first and foremost. Self-Love means you love yourself as God, your Creator, loves you, without any conditions, exclusions, or limitations.

It's a difficult place to get to, though, but the Twin Flame Journey is exceptionally helpful (if not *the vehicle)* in getting you there. Through the trials and triggers of your Journey, you will be able to shed all that is not *of* pure love. You will shed all that is *conditional* love. Everything will be stripped away and laid bare, and guess what still stands? Your *unconditional* love for yourself. But in order to also reach this state, it will be necessary for you to shed all your Limiting Beliefs about yourself, all the things that hold you back, that have held you back, all the excuses you've made, and continue making. By the time you get to this stage, you may not "need" your Twin Flame or the connection quite as much, but you will occasionally still feel the "pull" of him or her and the energy.

Sovereignty

Sovereignty is your declaration that you are a whole and sovereign being with defined borders and boundaries that are not to be crossed. As a sovereign being, you are not a "slave;" you are not "beholden", and you are not an instrument to anyone else. Your rights are just as important as anyone else's rights. Your wishes, your dreams, your desires, they are just as important. You will not subjugate yourself or make yourself secondary to anyone, under any circumstance. That which you have tolerated, you will no longer tolerate. You are the Emperor. You are the Empress. You are of the Divine, a divine light being, ordained, willed by God, to exist. You will not accept any treatment from anyone that is "less than." You will never deserve to be talked down to, to be talked about, to be looked down upon, to be emotionally or verbally abused, to be struck. You will always have access to your free will and your free will is a Universal Law that is incontrovertible. You are sovereign; you are whole.

Once you have successfully achieved and mastered these two states and ways of being, then you will begin to see your life change in amazing and some would say, miraculous, ways.

The Twin Flame Journey helps us to shed old, outdated karmic and ancestral patterns and societal programming that is not conducive to your greatest and highest good. All that is not of self-love, all that is not allowing you to exist as a sovereign being, you will begin to recognize these things, as a natural outcome of the Journey. In this way, these limiting patterns will be exposed and made conscious to you so that you can correct or adjust things, situations, circumstances, people, and relationship dynamics as needed so that you can internalize and embody these two critical Soul Lessons.

Accountability

One of the things that is important to keep in mind on the Twin Flame Journey is the concept of accountability. Accountability in the Journey has many facets, and I will touch on a few of them here. Some (perhaps a few) people "use" the Twin Flame concept or label as a reason to have an affair with their Twin outside of another existing relationship, or as a means to disregard another couple's commitment to one another, whether it is a marriage or not.

This is not okay. The 3-D bonds, commitments, and vows are important, also, and are part of your Divine Counterpart's life lessons and soul plan. When we act in a way that is not of integrity and not of the light, that can generate karma for both you and your Twin that will come up to be balanced out later. Running off into the sunset for love is somewhat of a romantic ideal in our reality, but it's not good when there is a spouse and/or children involved.

It's better to "do it clean" and handle things in a way that is "above board" and with integrity. This means being honest in your interactions with your Twin and their significant other (or yours) to the highest extent possible. This also means being honest if you are the one in the existing relationship.

Truly, if you find each other, and if you are true Twins, it is important to honor existing commitments with partners or spouses (and children), but if you find that the relationship you are in no longer serves you on a Soul Growth level, then it is important to get out of the relationship in a honest and straightforward way that is fueled by the intention of love and being in integrity.

Another aspect of accountability on the Journey is when there are things that happen regarding either Twin in relationship to the other. Sometimes runners and even chasers might do something that is not "above board" to your Twin. An example would be not being in integrity with your Twin…not telling the truth to your Twin (for whatever reason), and not taking responsibility for all the dust the Twin Flame Journey will inevitably kick up all around the two of you. One Twin should not have to shoulder it alone, but sadly, that is what sometimes happens. In every interaction, please try to be as honest and straightforward as possible, while also coming from the heart, and not from the ego. Saying "I am sorry" or "I was wrong" is not a sign of weakness; it's actually a noble expression of character and it can be very healing.

Likewise, offering forgiveness is equally noble and it's important that both Twins be able to do that when it is asked (and even when it isn't).

The bottom line is that the Twin Flame Journey asks us (no, actually, it requires of us) to be the highest expression of our true, authentic selves. This includes integrity and taking accountability. It means owning your share of it all. After all, when it gets down to it, the two Twins *did* actually co-create all of it, the entire experience, when you were mapping out your life experience and Soul Growth lessons. All of it is a lesson, an opportunity for learning, and we won't always get it right the first time, but over time, we will get better and better at these lessons.

Act in truth and integrity. Act out of love. Be the light.

Letting Go

Many of the steps and stages in the Twin Flame Journey can be excruciatingly difficult, and yet, there is one that was harder for me than the others. And that was the process of surrendering or letting go.

After being rebuffed by my Twin Flame (or the person I thought was my true Twin Flame) no fewer than five times, out of self-preservation and the effort to try to hold on to a shred of my own sanity and dignity (as well as the human need to have some sort of normalcy in my life and to move on and move forward and begin expanding my circle of friends and other romantic horizons), I made the difficult decision to let go and move on. I've found it to be a layered process. There were times I thought I had truly let go, only to find that there was still a shred of hope living inside. And then I would peel back the layers of the onion only to see there was more letting go to be had.

I was out boating with a friend and her family recently. One of the family members, former military, boarded the boat with a large, scripted tattoo across his chest: "Let go and let God." I had always found that to be a sort of well-meaning, but somewhat trite cliché, but it hit me across my own chest like a load of bricks.

In these various states of suffering, that is all you can do: Let go and truly ask God to take this suffering from you. In these same conversations with God, it's also good to ask Him to take over your Journey, take over the future of it, take over the worrying about it, take over the countless signs and symbols that come every day to remind you of it. And in that space of letting go and easing into your new life (whatever that may present for you, whether your Twin Flame is involved and included, or not), perhaps it is possible to foster your own continued healing and find peace. *(Psssttt...I am definitely healing, but I'll let you know how that works out and whether peace can truly be found.)*

(Author's Note: Late July 2020. Peace **can** *be found. Especially in nature, and also when you ask for "peace, harmony, and balance" daily.)*

Redemption

One of the recurring themes that comes to me as I write this from my retreat in the Blue Ridge Mountains of Virginia (as me and my children hunker down in a spot that is geographically remote due to concerns over COVID-19) is the Biblical concept of redemption. Redemption is a theme also found in many other world religions.

God will certainly put us through the fire, but He does so in order that we can be purified in the holiest of ways. The suffering, however, is not for naught...meaning it serves a purpose. A very holy purpose.

God reminds us so many times throughout the Bible (I am referring only to the Bible here because it is the text with which I am most familiar) of the concept of redemption. In fact, this theme is mentioned in this ancient text countless times.

From John 10:28-29: "And I give them eternal life, and they shall never perish; neither shall anyone snatch them out of my hand. My Father, who has given *them* to Me, is greater than all; and no one is able to snatch *them* out of my Father's hand."

And from Isaiah 54:4: "Do not fear, for you will not be ashamed; Neither be disgraced, for you will not be put to shame; For you will forget the shame of your youth." And Isaiah 54:7 says, "For a mere moment, I have forsaken you, but with great mercies I will gather you. With a little wrath I hid My face from you for a moment; but with everlasting kindness I will have mercy on you."

Though on your Journey and on your spiritual path to awakening, you have suffered and you have stumbled, and you most likely have fallen to your knees asking what is this, and when will the suffering end, God is with you and promises that love will win and "love will conquer all" (in the immortal words of Lionel Richie), and that your love for your Beloved was not for nothing. Think about it: Nothing in nature is wasted. You and your love that you feel so deeply within your heart, within your soul, are of nature, so in loving another, that love is never wasted, and never will be. Your unconditional love for another is noted, duly noted, by the Heavens and even God Himself and it will not be for naught.

Communicating With Your Twin's Higher Spirit/Higher Self

In Book One of *The Twin Flame Guidebook*, we talked about using telepathy to communicate with your Twin's Higher Self. No matter what's going on with your actual Twin in the 3-D world, your Twin's Higher Spirit is always divine and always grounded into the Higher Realms (5-D and beyond) and is not (and won't be caught up) in the petty affairs of this world. (Meaning, no triggers will result from your communication with him or her in the Higher Realms.)

In addition to this method as described in that first book, you can also communicate directly with your Twin's Higher Self and that can be particularly helpful during a long period of Separation, or in a "no contact" situation where your Twin has asked you not to contact him or her.

Obviously, the need for one Twin to communicate with the other is sometimes great and the pull to do so can feel like a giant magnet. At times, though, one of the Twins may not want communication, for whatever reasons, and that is okay.

You can simply reach out to your Twin's Higher Self using the following steps:

1) Ground yourself with meditation or time in nature.

2) Set the intention to communicate with your Twin's Higher Self (remember intention is everything!)

3) Using simple, straightforward language, "say what you need to say." (In the immortal words of John Mayer.) This could be a prayer for your Divine Counterpart, this could be an apology, or this could be an offer of forgiveness. You can even do the ho'oponopono prayer described on page 4 of this book.

4) You can then confirm the message was received by your Twin using your own higher guidance and/or intuition, or by using a pendulum to confirm. That message will then find a way into the Twin's 3-D consciousness and he or she may be more accepting of the message.

Often, this approach can be helpful as you try to work through the stickier, messier parts of the Journey. Remember, the connection is always there, and the communication never really ceases, though it may appear that way in the regular, obvious, and tangible 3-D world. As Lee Patterson once told me, much to my surprise: "Remember, she can *hear* you!" The energy you two share is ever-present and omni-directional, meaning it always surrounds you and it will never go away. The truth is, if you are true Twins, you'll never be separated by silence, by time, by miles, or distance (even including emotional distance).

The Two Little Birds Return

I deeply value my Native American heritage and ancestry and from researching my heritage, I have learned how much we look to the animal kingdom for signs and symbols from our Creator to guide us on our paths and in our daily lives. One such sign showed up while I was writing Book One of *The Twin Flame Guidebook*.

In that book I talked about two little sparrows who came into my pool cage, and despite impossible odds, they always seemed to find their way out of the cage. They kept returning, time and again, and I would think I had to help them escape, but no, they always came together as a pair, and they always found a way out (or a way through) together.

So, just a few weeks ago (as I write this), the two little sparrows had returned, and I noticed they were scouting out a terra cotta planter on the exterior wall of the home for some reason.

Turns out the two little birds were looking for and building a home for a nest for their soon-to-be-born little chicks. The sparrow parents diligently built their nest every day, bringing small scraps of pine needles, cloth, and twigs to make a comfy little nest for their little ones.

A couple of weeks later, my kids and I could hear the little birds making a cheep-cheep sound in the nest and awaiting their Mom and Dad Sparrows to bring them food. A few weeks later, the little ones learned to fly and were off on their own adventures in what must seem like a very big world to them.

My point is, the parent sparrows came home as I was writing Book Two, they built a nest, and they built a life together. Their little co-created babies had a beautiful and safe little home and nest, and their lives unfolded just as they should, per the Divine Plan.

If all these small birds are a sign from the Universe for me and for all of us, let us accept it and find our own meaning in it. For me, it means we are always divinely guided and protected and we can relax as our lives unfold naturally and organically, in the most precious and delicious of ways.

The Mysterious Gold Thread

In *The Twin Flame Guidebook: Your Practical Guide to Navigating the Journey: Book One*, we talked about the mysterious red thread, the red thread of fate. I'll include the synopsis here for your convenience, though in a shortened form.

> The Red Thread of Fate, also referred to as the Red Thread of Marriage, and other variants, is an Asian belief originating from Chinese legend. According to this myth, the gods tie an invisible red cord around the ankles of those who are destined to meet one another in a certain situation or help each other in a certain way. Often, in Japanese and Korean culture, it is thought to be tied around the little finger. According to Chinese legend, the deity in charge of "the red thread" is believed to be Yuè Xià Lǎorén, often abbreviated to Yuè Lǎo, the old lunar matchmaker god, who is in charge of marriages.

> The two people connected by the red thread are destined lovers, regardless of place, time, or circumstances. This magical cord may stretch or tangle, but never break. This myth is similar to the Western concept of soulmate or a destined Twin Flame.

The red thread is also tied to the Jewish Kabbalah, a mystical belief system and a red thread is tied around your left wrist to offer you protection against negative energy (or in the olden days, as it was called, "the evil eye.")

(Cited from Wikipedia)

In this book on the cover, you'll see a different thread, but this time, a golden one.

This gold thread is the divine thread of God, the color of divinity, which is where this Journey brings us, back to the divine. Based on one story from Greek mythology, Queen Pasiphaë gave her son, Zeus, the magical thread to assist him on his heroic journey into the labyrinth, which is representative of life.

In yet another story, Ariadne gives her Beloved, the hero-warrior Theseus, a thread that was said to be silver to help guide him through the same labyrinth. At the center of the labyrinth, there is a half-bull, half-man minotaur. As part of Theseus' Hero's Journey, he had to kill the terrifying minotaur and find his way back out of the maze again, using the "shiny breadcrumb trail" given him by Ariadne: the golden thread.

In our own personal Journeys, the labyrinth can be viewed as the Twin Flame Journey, and the scary Minotaur as anything that obstructs our path to Union with our Twin, or our own inner Self-Union. The creature can also be viewed as Limiting Beliefs holding you back from the things you want to do and the path you want to pursue. Once the monster is slain, then you follow the golden thread provided by your Beloved, back to either him or her, or your own Union with Self, and your own Union with the Divine. No matter the end result, you come out of the Journey a more perfect, more divine, more whole version of yourself, with vastly unlimited potential.

At the beginning of our own Hero's Journey, we think we can just state what we most desire and go get it; however, the Universe/God/Source Energy has its own plans, and it doesn't always work out in the way we think or need (or want). Some of us, at times, may try to "force" things to go the way we want, to suit our own needs, and we can be very inflexible. The golden thread, representing your intuition and inspiration that guides your Soul Growth, draws you back to the Divine Mind and Divine Will, where things may play out differently than you might think, but always for your (and your Twin's) best and highest good.

"As we travel through literal and figurative labyrinths in our lives, the golden thread may easily go unnoticed, yet when it is recognized and followed, we may find that this archetypal strand of gold connects us to our true selves, to our beloveds, and to that which we discover to be home."

(Source: Stellamara and Patrick Queen, via www.sophias-children.com)

Supplemental reading/research suggestion:
As part of your reading and research, be sure to check out Joseph Campbell's "Hero's Journey," which is the Journey of

each of us, of every one of us, a journey which is so often captured in some of the most famous books and movies including Tolkien's *The Hobbit/Lord of the Rings* series and Lucas' *Star Wars* series.

K Moon, Western astrologer and Twin Flame intuitive, talks about this a bit on her YouTube channel. Check her out, if you can.

How Will Twin Flames Change the World?

The truth is, we just don't yet know how Twin Flames will change the world, but enough early indicators are there to start making some educated guesses.

For one, they are beginning to show people close to them (family, friends, acquaintances) the meaning of true, unconditional love and how it is expressed by how awakened Twins "show up" in the world and the close relationships that an awakened Twin has...and the way in which he or she behaves in the world (including how he or she reacts to circumstances and events and how she or he interacts with other people). They are beginning to show anyone who knows them that separation is only an illusion and that we are all interconnected to one another and to Spirit.

In terms of karmic relationships, in my own personal relationship with my karmic partner, even she is doing research on her own (as a result of all we've been through) and is beginning to understand the concepts. Last night, she even expressed to me the intention of not relying on other people quite so much, not having so many people "carry her water." For the first time, I saw tears in her eyes in relation to how she has, at times, treated other people over time and for lack of a better term, used them in some way for her own means, with no reciprocal return back to them for the help or assistance. I saw some sadness and compunction in her face over how she had been interacting with many people over the years, and the irony that was not lost on me, was that I was perhaps number one on that list of people.

When I allow my thoughts to get more fanciful, though, I imagine (and it's very likely based on what I've seen and my own experience) a world that no longer needs divorce attorneys and possibly a world that no longer needs therapists (as just two examples). Because we Twins, through our own personal Journeys and struggles, have learned how to effectively acknowledge, heal, purge, and transmute "negative" emotions, such as self-doubt, blame, shame, sadness, victim mentality, power dynamics, and distorted expressions of both the Divine Feminine and Divine Masculine. In fact, when asked, I often give advice to some close to me, leveraging my own experience and perspectives on the Journey and it always seems well-received. The person is usually like, "I hadn't thought about it like that."

So, even on purely an interpersonal level, we are greatly impacting those around us. Our interactions with those around us will ripple out in ways we cannot even begin to understand or see, like a pebble being tossed into a body of water and the concentric circles that emanate out from it. One act of kindness...one act of understanding...exhibiting patient endurance in a particular situation...demonstrating grace...expressing forgiveness...then multiplies to the interaction that person will have with another, and then, so it goes...to another, and then to another, until it becomes exponential.

Just imagine a newer, better, safer, and more peaceful world with less conflict and fighting (more peace), less friction (more, many, or all people getting along), less domination (more people rising into their own sovereignty) and more self-understanding and more self-love (as within, so without). That self-understanding and self-love transforms a person from the inside out, and that subsequently changes how he or she interacts in the world.

It's possible, if enough of us get this right (and do our work and fulfill our missions that we set out to do even before we incarnated on this Earth), we may actually end up making this world better than we found it. It may not always be perfect, but it will be so much better. Loving and honoring our fellow humans (just think: Fewer wars and less unnecessary destruction and killing, caring for and protecting children and adolescents, as well as all the beautiful species and resources of this planet, nurturing and defending Mother Earth and the environment she provides us to live, grow, and thrive, as a few examples.)

Loving ourselves, loving others, loving our home planet. It's all possible. We just have to do our work, share our experiences and insight, BELIEVE, and be what we believe in, in every instance and every interaction. That's how we change the world, one word, one action, one belief, one random act of kindness, one prayer, at a time.

Thank you for joining me on this excellent Journey. I wish you much peace and love. Until we meet again...

The Twin Flame Guidebook 2 Playlist

If you're like me, music is a huge part of your life, and a big part of my personal coping mechanism. Really good music can help keep your vibration high when you are feeling low on your Journey. The following songs were my companions as I wrote this second guidebook, and I feel they reflect the phases of the Journey discussed in this book. (Please note: I am a child of the 70s and 80s, so this playlist largely reflects those decades.) Find the music that moves your heart and soul and brings you the "warm fuzzies." There are so many great songs and in retrospect to me, every love song is a Twin Flame song; these are just a few of my current faves.

- "A Taste of Honey" by Sukiyaki
- "Ain't No Sunshine" by Melody Gardot
- "All for You" by Janet Jackson
- "All I Need" by Radiohead
- "Bad Time" by Grand Funk Railroad
- "Biggest Part of Me" by Ambrosia
- "Clarity" by John Mayer
- "Constant Craving" by k.d. lang
- "Cuts You Up" by Peter Murphy
- "Everybody's Got to Learn Sometime" by The Korgis
- "Fool If You Think It's Over" by Chris Rea

- "Fortress Around Your Heart" by Sting
- "Give Me Love (Give Me Peace on Earth)" by George Harrison
- "Ghost" by the Indigo Girls
- "Hard Habit to Break" by Chicago
- "Heartbreak Warfare" by John Mayer
- "Here With Me" by Dido
- "Higher Love" by Steve Winwood
- "I Wish U Heaven" by Prince
- "It Might Be You" by Stephen Bishop
- "Just Remember I Love You" by Firefall
- "Let Me Call You Sweetheart" by Patti Page
- "Let Your Love Flow" by the Bellamy Brothers
- "Livin' On a Prayer" by Bon Jovi
- "Look Back in Anger" by David Bowie*
- "Love Touch" by Rod Stewart
- "Love Will Conquer All" by Lionel Richie
- "Missing You" by John Waite
- "Moonlight Feels Right" by Starbuck
- "Need You Tonight" by INXS
- "Night and Day" by U2
- "Nobody Told Me" by John Lennon
- "Nothing Compares 2 U" by Prince
- "Over the Wall" by Echo & The Bunnymen*
- "Que Sera Sera" by Doris Day
- "Save a Prayer" by Duran Duran
- "Slave to Love" by Bryan Ferry
- "So Alive" by Love and Rockets
- "Sweet Surrender" by Sarah McLachlan
- "Suddenly" by Olivia Newton John and Cliff Richard
- "Take a Picture" by Filter
- "Thank U" by Alanis Morissette

- "The Captain of Her Heart" by Double
- "The Second Time Around" by Shalamar
- "Tired of Being Alone" by Al Green
- "That's Life" by Frank Sinatra
- "The Edge of Heaven" by Wham!
- "Too Late for Goodbyes" by Julian Lennon
- "Too Late to Turn Back Now" by Cornelius Bros and Sister Rose
- "You Make Me Feel Like Dancin'" by Leo Sayer
- "Wake Up" by XTC*
- "We Found Love" by Rihanna (Featuring Calvin Harris)
- "What the World Needs Now" by Jackie DeShannon
- "White Flag" by Dido
- "You Ain't Seen Nothing Yet" by Bachman Turner Overdrive
- "You Make Me Feel Like Dancin'" by Leo Sayer
- "'65 Love Affair" by Paul Davis

*Obscure, 80s alternative songs that will probably only make sense to me and have meaning for me, the author ;)

Twin Flame Prayer (by K.D. Courage, as Channeled by her Spiritual Guides)

God, please anoint me and my Beloved in love so that we may be a light in the world.

God, Lord, please anoint us in health.

In peace...

In balance...

In harmony...

So that we may fulfill your Divine Will, for the greatest and highest good.

Amen.

Questions and Answers About the Twin Flame Journey

(Please reference Book One of *The Twin Flame Guidebook: Your Practical Guide to the Journey* for more questions and answers that you can also find on Quora, one of the other platforms that I use frequently.)

Can you dream of your Twin Flame prior to meeting him or her?

Yes, I do believe that many of us dream of our Twins prior to meeting them. In my case, this is true. Following below, an excerpt from my real-life experience in the dreamscape:

Sometime between 2014 and 2016, I had a very, very real dream, a dream I've later learned meets all the requirements of a "lucid dream," which essentially means the dream is super-realistic and you can consciously think about (and realize you are) thinking and making decisions in the dream (which is a relatively new thing for me).

During this dream, I met an incredible person, a beautiful female with blonde hair, who I knew immediately was a soul mate or possibly something more. She was definitely a lover, and her love for me that she expressed in that dream, both in words and in actions, was beyond any love I have ever felt in my waking, 3-D lifetime. The connection and feeling I felt was heads above anything (beyond the most intimate, beyond the most magnetic) I had ever experienced before.

This dream of the woman later became a recurring dream, but when I first had it, when I awoke, I missed her so terribly and I was upset to wake up. I wanted to get that connection back, get that ethereal feeling back. It was the greatest feeling of love, specifically, unconditional love, that I had ever felt in my life.

— From *The Twin Flame Guidebook: Your Practical Guide to Navigating the Journey (Book One) by K.D. Courage*

What if only you are experiencing Twin Flame signs and she or he isn't?

Well, this sounds as if you are what is known as the "awakened twin" and perhaps she is not. Some people argue about these semantics, but I will go with a simple answer. It's quite possible: A) You are Twin Flames, and B) That you are the awakened one. Just because you aren't aware (or aren't being told) that she is experiencing signs and synchronicities, it doesn't mean that she isn't.

Many "unawakened" Twins will deny the connection or will "run" from it. It surfaces many emotions in them that they may not be ready to deal with. One Twin is usually the "awakened" one and is usually considered the "chaser." The one who denies the connection, or runs, is typically called the "runner." Sometimes these roles will change or flex over time; for example, the chaser later becomes the runner (and vice versa).

One of the most important things to know is that if you are true Twins, then you are co-creating your current reality to surface in both you and her the wounds that need acknowledgement and healing. Oftentimes, these wounds are rejection, abandonment, lack of self-worth, etc. She will "trigger" you, you will "trigger" her, running and chasing will commence (in a "typical" Twin Flame Journey).

Can you explain the perspective of the "chaser" Twin Flame?

My Twin "ignited" or "activated" me (seemingly unwittingly or subconsciously) on a summer night. Over time, it became clear that this person was a significant and meaningful soul connection to me. I eventually expressed my emotions to this person. This person, who had previously shown interest in different ways (at least based on my perception), rejected my interest. I was in an almost 20-year relationship with another person (and was raising two kids with this partner) and there were many obstacles and real-world dynamics working against me and my Twin. Fast forward: Many push-pull and triggering dynamics over a multi-year span. Usually with me expressing emotion and being honest and my Twin not being honest, hiding feelings, suppressing feelings, avoiding contact. And then blocking between us: First me blocking my Twin on social media, then her blocking me, and so on and so forth. It's obvious from some limited contact now that we have both grown exponentially, we still care for the other, but despite me leaving my then-partner, my Twin and I are currently in another Separation (I detail those steps of the process or the path in Book One of *The Twin Flame Guidebook: Your Practical Guide to Navigating the Journey*).

Why does an awakened Twin Flame run? If they are aware of the divinity in the connection, they don't run for the usual reasons, so what would they run from? Is it because it is a necessity for the unawakened chaser to experience the abandonment?

First off, I think it's hard to determine who's awakened, or not, and when. For example, I thought I was the first "awakened" Twin, but it's possible my Twin may have awakened first. I am just not sure and only time will tell. I will caution all Twins to be careful of the thought process, "Oh, I am awakened" and "he [or she] is not." We just cannot know and likely won't know until our Journey unfolds further and we can actually have these types of conversations with our Twins.

But, to answer the rest of your question...

Every Twin Flame "couple" is different, and their experience is different. Sometimes it's the Divine Feminine who runs and sometimes the roles switch over time, with the Twins alternating between the "runner" and "chaser" roles. But there are often commonalities among all Twins. I will write the answer to this question from my own perspective.

I am not a "runner," (as far as I know), but I will do my best to address why certain Twin Flames run, as I understand it, from everything I have personally experienced and everything I have read and heard on the Journey (and the experiences of many friends). Many say they run because the Twin Flame connection is too intense. It brings up too much in their emotional field: too much doubt, too many questions. Also, they feel they're not ready for such a "big love." They're not ready to experience such intense emotions and the deep spiritual connection. In fact, some of them may not be ready for any type of real love, or authentic love. He or she may have gotten used to the 3-D templates of love and sex and that is all they have learned to expect. A new experience, or the potential of a new experience, perhaps "blows their minds" and they don't know what to do with it, how to categorize it, or how to understand it. They may not be ready for the connection. This Journey cannot be understood with the rational mind or logic, but rather, only with the heart and the heart's logic.

"Runners" may also flee and block you because of certain 3-D realities, such as when you have a partner, a spouse, kids, a family. It may be too messy or inconvenient to disrupt (or seemingly disrupt) a family unit that is on the outside, by all accounts, a "happy family." [In retrospect, I am grateful to my Twin for blocking me because it helped me face and heal some key and persistent core wounds of mine, and it also enabled me to process and heal without any additional co-dependency on my Twin – or anyone. It also provided a healing process and environment free of distractions.]

On the path of the Twins, there can also be family issues or obstacles that surface, like perhaps the concern that relationship won't be accepted by the Twin's family (or Twins' families) because of things like the gender, race, religion or other cultural differences, or the socioeconomic status of their Twin, or the age difference between him or her and the Twin.

Another key factor of why Twins sometimes run is because they may associate the karma and karmic lessons that come as a result of the Journey, with their Divine Counterpart. It may appear to them that she (or he) caused it all, or that she is at fault, or that she did something to bring all of this upon the both of them when, in fact, it is a collaborative Journey and a collaborative, co-creative "project" between the two Twins for the benefit of both of them. This co-creation is designed so that both souls can experience these karmic lessons and process through them so that they can both resolve issues and achieve true Soul Growth.

The truth is we Twin Flames mirror one another perfectly and we "trigger" one another perfectly; it is that way by design. Self-growth and self-development are never "fun," nor are they easy. This is not a comfortable process for many (or most), and so they may wish to avoid it. I think both my Twin and I have experienced these triggers and in truth, wished to avoid the process of self-growth, but after more time and introspection, I wouldn't have traded our experience (so far) for the world, even despite the pain and suffering I (and she) have experienced. It helped me grow. It helped me expand, and for that I will forever be grateful as I believe it was part of my Soul Purpose and Soul Mission to grow and expand in this 3-D lifetime, in this incarnation, in the exact way that I did (as a result of the Journey).

These obstacles, while huge, are not insurmountable, as many Twins in Union can attest. Sometimes it requires a miracle, or many miracles, but if you're like me, you believe in miracles. You've seen them firsthand. This Journey is no different.

One valuable thing you may wish to do is to look up the Twins in Union videos by K. Moon (Western astrologer and Twin Flame intuitive/teacher) on YouTube. You'll hear firsthand of the trials and tribulations of these Twin couples, but most important, you'll get to hear "the why" of why it all happened the way it did.

In the Twin Flame experience, does chasing mean one really does not trust the connection?

I think chasing **DOES** equal not really trusting the connection. I cover this topic in my first book (*The Twin Flame Guidebook*) in the chapter entitled: "Why We Chase and Why We Run."

Why do we chase? It's an important question to ask yourself if you're a Divine Feminine, and I've only been able to answer it after several years of being on this Journey.

I believe we, as Divine Feminines, chase our Twin, our Divine Counterpart, because we are so acclimated to the typical 3-D approach to love and relationships. To obtain love, we believe we must court it, we must follow our emotions to their natural equivalent of actions to cement the connection, to try to "make it real." We then try to "wrestle it to the ground." But on the Twin Flame Journey, things don't work as they do in the 3-D, and your usual methods that work so well to attract someone to you and to keep them there, don't work at all, much to your dismay.

Many of us are so desperate for true love and affection, that when we think we sense it, we run toward it with all our energy and all our might. We will do practically anything to try to make it real (at least, as real as it is in our own hearts and minds.)

I also believe we chase because we are not confident in our own skins. We do not love ourselves in a sufficient way, and so we are always seeking love from somewhere outside of us, just like we are always seeking validation outside of us. We don't yet know that true love and true acceptance starts with ourselves, and we must love ourselves wholly and completely first before anyone else can—or will. We must feel whole inside of ourselves before we can join with another.

Another fact about chasing is that we do it as a form of (attempted) control. It's just the truth of the matter. I think perhaps I didn't want to admit this to myself for a long time, but it finally came to me recently that it is another way for us to try to control our Divine Partner, to try to control the Journey, to make ourselves feel more comfortable, to exert some power over a situation that makes us feel powerless. Once we recognize this fact and admit it, then we can start the process of true surrender and release, and "get out of our own ways" so that everything can unfold naturally, in Divine Timing.

I also sense that we chase on the Journey (time and again) to keep it feeling "real." We want our Twin Flame to acknowledge the connection, to admit they feel the same way that we do. We feel we must accomplish this above all else (again, as proof of the connection).

Can one Twin Flame be "way ahead" on the Journey, while the other has not put in the work?

I believe your question is built on a false notion or assumption...that your Twin Flame isn't "putting in the work," though I completely understand and have experienced that feeling or belief myself. The truth is, you are both co-creating the entire experience based on your agreed-upon soul contracts well before you incarnated on Earth in this lifetime. You are in this completely together, and even when it feels he or she is not participating, I can assure you they are, from the higher realms/higher self, or in the dreamspace. They may also be (unbeknownst to you) helping you clear your own internal blocks, false beliefs, and limiting and self-defeating behaviors.

I think you will come to see, over time, that your Twin has been—and is—right there with you all along. Even when you feel your most lonely and most abandoned, he or she is actually right there with you.

What about Catalyst, or False, Twins? Do they exist?

Everyone has a right to their own opinions and beliefs, but I personally don't believe in a Catalyst, or False Twin, and my divination sources agree. I know others who also say this does not exist. If you are a Twin, and it's not always "hunky-dory" or unicorns and rainbows, that is okay.

The triggering…it's all part of balancing out the karma from your current experience with your Twin and also past lives. The point is, your Twin will trigger your wounds perfectly, and you will do so for them, as well. Once the unconscious is made conscious, it's up to you to do the healing work, and to transmute it. It's a co-creative process between you and your Twin on several different dimensional levels. It's not meant to be easy. And it's not meant to be smooth.

Twin Flames are not the same as soulmates. If you walk away before the work is done, then you've missed some Soul Growth opportunities.

If you feel you are on this path or this wave, a great YouTube reader to try is Sylvia Escalante at The Enchanted World of Twin Flame. She's on Facebook, YouTube, and numerous other social media platforms. She always serves it up to us, straight, with no chaser...the good, the bad, and the ugly.

Why is it so difficult to let go of and release my Twin Flame when I realize that I need to?

When you are ready, you will be able to detach and let go, and in fact, this is a necessary part/step in the Journey, as it seems you are aware.

Detachment means you are able to release any expectations of your Twin Flame and hopes for a certain outcome. As human beings, detachment is very difficult, but we can get there. When you realize the Universe/Source Energy has your best interest at heart, no matter what, then you can relax in the faith that you are safe, everything is handled, and God/ Source Energy/Universe may have even something greater in store for you than you can see, imagine, or realize.

Yes, it's true. We all long to be reunited with our Twin Flames. And in time, that may happen if we have done our work and found peace, satisfaction, and contentment inside ourselves. When we find unconditional love for our own selves, then it becomes irrelevant who else loves you. It's a "nice-to-have" if someone else does (of course), but you come to realize you no longer need anyone else's love, respect, admiration, validation, or approval. You have it all inside yourself, and that is perhaps the greatest gift of the Journey.

What needs to be done to own the Twin Flame Union from within (accepting the Union and not going back and forth with energies) in order to attract it into reality?

I think the answer to this one is SURRENDER. It is also very important, if not critical, to try to balance your masculine and feminine energies within you, to shed distorted masculine and feminine energies, and to become fully empowered in both those divine Emperor/Empress energies. It means both standing in your truth and in your own authority, and also, it means getting in touch with your emotional side and balancing it all out within yourself. It also includes releasing any old energetic blocks or karma and healing from past wounds and traumas. When all this is said and done, then you get closer to that pre-Union/Union energy. And I will add, when you reach this stage, you no longer NEED your Twin Flame, though you may occasionally long for them and want them in your life. But it's no longer a deep and burning need because you have become complete and whole within yourself. Because you are complete within yourself, then you become ready for Divine Union.

While in separation from my Twin Flame, I am having scenarios of a date coming into my thoughts, and the same with dreams. Could you explain?

I assume you are meaning you are having scenarios or thoughts of a date with your Twin coming through, as well as many dreams. This is consistent with the Twin Flame experience, with lots of images, visions, impressions, etc. coming through especially during times of Separation. Even though you are in Separation, the connection between you and your Beloved never severs. You are constantly in each other's energy field. You can actually feel and sometimes "hear" your Twin's thoughts. I know it sounds far-fetched, but this has been well-documented within the Twin Flame community (especially those Twins in Union).

The dreamspace is where you and your Twin will "communicate" in word, action, and deed, for now. In the dreamscape, you will have valuable insights into your connection, what may be blocking your connection, and how your Twin really feels about you despite how they may be acting in the "real world," or the 3-D.

Just like when you look out over the ocean and see very little activity on the surface, there is a whole universe teeming with life underneath. Often, there is far more than meets the eye going on with your connection. How things "seem" is not always the case.

Use the time in Separation to work on self-love of yourself and self-growth, assisting your fellow humans in the way that you can, sharing your God-given gifts, and enjoying life. Everything will come together and happen as it's supposed to, in Divine Timing, whether it's Union or furthering the growth and development of your own soul.

Why is there an 11:11 time stamp on the picture I took with my Twin Flame? Is it a validation?

Yes, it very well could be and if you think it is, it most likely is! In "TwinFlameLand," we call this a "synch" (or a synchronicity). Here are some meanings behind the number 11:11, based on my research.

- 11:11 is "The Twin Flame Number"
- A master number
- The bigger picture
- The Divine Path
- Represents the "code of activation"
- Take a breath, quiet your mind, and listen to the messages that source energy has for you now
- Shows evidence of alignment with God, Universe, spirit
- Connection between humans and God, Universe, spirit
- An auspicious sign
- Oneness; unity
- Angels or spirit guides are close by
- You are a divine aspect of the Creator
- A reminder that you came here for a purpose and to leave the Earth better than you found it when you were born
- Tremendous opportunities
- A new path is opening up for you
- Be aware and open to blessings
- A wake-up call of divine intervention
- You are guided, supported, and loved
- A reminder to raise your vibration

- Confirms your ability to manifest rapidly
- A reminder to pay attention to your thoughts
- A gentle nudge to stay positive
- Encouragement to couple your unique gifts with that of your Twin to also help raise the vibration of humanity and Earth.

Will your Twin Flame lie to you?

I hate to answer this question in the affirmative, but based on my own personal experience, I do believe your Twin Flame may deceive you. I am not sure whether he or she does it intentionally, but I do believe my Twin has lied to me or misled me upon many occasions about her feelings for me (or lack thereof), or where she "is" in life (everything is always "hunky-dory" when I perceive otherwise). Of course, when your own intuition is telling you what they are saying is not true, it's easy to doubt yourself when you're looking eye to eye with him or her. But what I've also discovered on this Journey, is that when I check for confirmation in various ways, it typically points to the fact that my Twin is not being 100% honest. I believe most of what this is about is related to our Twin's fears regarding the "Big Love," of not being ready for it, perhaps not being worthy of it, or perhaps because of fear of losing control. It can also be related to the "masks" the Twin will wear, the false personas. These are all valid reasons for which people will (and do) lie.

The challenge for Twins, I think, is to be authentic, and to stand in your own truth and your own authority as much as is humanly possible. We can, in essence, "light the way" for our Twins.

How can I distract myself from daydreaming about my Twin Flame who is already married with kids?

I've found it's somewhat impossible to distract yourself during certain periods of the Twin Flame Journey. In the beginning, like, say, the first few years, you'll find that you cannot stop thinking about your person and you'll lose count of the times that the person pops into your head, day and night. When you wake up, thoughts of them will be on your mind, all throughout the day, and before bed at night. It's not something you try to do; it just is! It's a spiritual connection and therefore, it is very strong.

Once you have been on the Journey for a few years, you will be able to master your thoughts more and exert more control, and you will also have other things you are working on, like your mission work (what your soul intended to do or a purpose you sought to fulfill before you even incarnated in the 3-D dimensional realm), and that will distract you. I am fully into my mission work now (my Twin and I are in a deep Separation, one of many), and so I have "thrown myself" into other things and that has helped greatly.

The matter of a Twin in another involved, committed relationship (even marriage) with kids is one I know well, having been in that role of the committed person myself. These instances are very difficult, but if the two of you are meant to come together in Divine Union, you will. If God wills it, there is nothing that can stand in its way. But with that said, you should be sure to conduct yourself in such a way that you are acting in truth, honesty, and integrity. You want to avoid incurring any "negative" karma along the way. Just be sure to be OF the light and to act OF the light, and all will work out just as it's supposed to. We must all remember this Journey may not necessarily mean a physical relationship with our Twin in the 3-D world. It may... that is a possibility, but just remember no matter if you are "together," or not, you are still co-creating with your Twin and his/her Higher Self in the higher realms.

Reviews

If you enjoyed this book or found it helpful along your Journey, please leave a positive review on Amazon, Barnes & Noble, or wherever (or however) you're reading this. I would also appreciate positive reviews on Goodreads, if you're on that platform. Thank you in advance!

About Twin Crows Publishing House, a Division of Twin Crows Media

Twin Crows Publishing House is born of two crows, twins. It takes two to make a perfect complement, a perfect Union. The two represent the yin and the yang, the balancing of equal energies. Two also represents a couple, the lovers.

Crows are our connection to the spiritual realms. They are able to bring messages from the higher to us on this 3-D plane. They are said to be perhaps the most spiritual of animals.

Our global publishing house is devoted to the lifting up of humanity, through increasing spiritual awareness and by elevating our collective consciousness. In this way, we can transcend earthly limitations, lack and fear, and bring about a new way of being, a new understanding, full of light, love, joy, happiness, abundance, prosperity and health for everyone.

We are deeply committed to assisting first-time and veteran authors in both fiction and non-fiction, new, up-and-coming authors, female authors, and authors who are focused in the areas of: Spirituality, self-growth, Soul Growth, empowerment, equality, love, human rights, peace, freedom, health and well-being, and the environment.

Twin Crows Publishing House is part of Twin Crows Media, a full-service, independent communications firm. Twin Crows Media specializes in helping influencers brand themselves and create and package their content and distribute it across an integrated platform that includes, but is not limited to: Books, blogs, social media, podcasts, online courses, online channels, retreats, conferences, workshops, printed materials, and more. We also offer photography services (both national and international). Just like the purpose of Twin Crows Publishing House, the end goal is the uplifting of humanity, one person at a time. Our core content areas include: Human rights (for all people), the emotional/spiritual/physical landscape, the environment, climate issues, and more. You can find us on Facebook at: Twin Crows Publishing House/Twin Crows Media.

About K.D. Courage

K.D. Courage is a Twin Flame and has been on the Journey for many years. A former corporate executive who started her career in publishing, K.D. now focuses her attention on using her gifts (spiritual and otherwise) to help men and women achieve a lighter, brighter, and better state of being. K.D. is a spiritual instructor and certified Reiki healer and has also authored pieces in books, websites, magazines, newspapers, newsweeklies, and literary magazines. In her spare time (when she's not writing, editing, or traveling), she's spending time with her family, creating art, doing photography, bicycling, swimming, and working on reviving her musical aspirations (always a work in progress). K.D. has worked with more than 40 non-profits and not-for-profits, serving on the boards of several of them and providing them with time, resources, funding, and space to help them support their missions. K.D.'s soul purpose is not only "purity" but "to become the perfect vessel for perfect love." While that sounds like a lofty goal, she believes it's 100% achievable.

K.D. invites you to email her at <u>twinflameguidebook@ gmail.com</u> and to please follow her and subscribe to her on Facebook at: K.D. Courage.

K.D. Courage is available for conferences, speaking engagements, and workshops across the globe. Please contact twinflameguidebook@gmail.com.

Other books by K.D. Courage

The Twin Flame Guidebook: Your Practical Guide to the Journey (Book One in the series)

Available on Amazon, Barnes & Noble and through Ingram (U.S.), Gardners (UK), and select retail outlets worldwide.

ISBN: 978-0-578-56460-9

Other Books Relative to the Twin Flame Journey

The Enchanted World of Twin Flame Book Series

The Enchanted World of Twin Flame book series by Sylvia (Sylvia Escalante) is the true story of the spiritual and emotional journey and intense physical connection of a nurse, Sylvia, who by circumstances of fate, meets a police officer, London. In this book, Sylvia takes us on a deeply personal spiritual (5-D) journey and its 3-D manifestations as she and London navigate their connection of pure love, with its extreme lows and exalting highs. In this book, you'll learn more about the nature of divine love and divine alchemy as exemplified by Ascended Masters as you follow Sylvia and London through their tumultuous and passion-filled Twin Flame Journey, a Journey to wholeness, unity, union with self, and ultimately, unconditional love. In book two, you'll enjoy a fast-paced read as Sylvia explores the Higher Realms with her spirit guides as they help her discover and uncover the mysteries of the Twin Flame Journey.

Her books have reached number one on Amazon within days of their release, and are a sought-out resource for people worldwide who are on a spiritual path.

About Sylvia

Sylvia is a popular channeler, Tarot reader, and two-time author focusing on Twin Flames and spirituality with more than 19,000 followers and 3.5 million views on YouTube, as well as thousands of followers on other social media platforms. Sylvia started her career as a nurse, but through the Twin Flame Journey, discovered her talents and passion for spiritual teaching as guided by her trusted guides and Ascended Masters. In her service to Twin Flames and humanity, Sylvia's objectives are to help people as they break their shackles and ascend the limitations of the ordinary 3-D world to realize their full potential, their divine essence, and their divine partnerships. She does this by sharing personal stories of her own enlightenment experience to bring about a greater awareness of spirituality, cosmic love, and cosmic consciousness. The end goal is a better, more joyful, more peaceful, more understanding world, powered by love. To contact Sylvia directly, please email: Twinflamereaders@gmail.com. Please also check out her platforms on social media, including YouTube under: The Enchanted World of Twin Flame.

Made in the USA
Monee, IL
17 October 2020